WHY IN AMERICA COMMON SENSE ISN'T SO COMMON

SIMPLE FIXES FOR AMERICA'S ABSURDITIES

SAINT MAHA KAAL

Plutus Publishers

First Edition, 2024

ISBN: 9798330205301 (print)
ISBN: 9798330205318 (ebook)

To everyone who has ever been bothered by the absurdities and injustices in our world.

And to those who seek common sense where it seems to be lacking. This book is for you.

Preface

This book is a collection of everyday puzzles that make you stop, scratch your head, and wonder, "What the heck is going on here?" Ever notice how your paper straw turns into mush before you're even halfway through your smoothie? Or how getting money from your own bank account feels like you're trying to break into a fortress? What about sitting in traffic and thinking, "Couldn't they fix these roads at night?"

In this book, we'll talk about all the bizarre, illogical, and downright annoying stuff we encounter every day. Each chapter in this book looks at the funny and sometimes annoying parts of everyday life that just don't seem to make sense—from the ridiculously high cost of hospital parking, to the agonizing complexities of school bureaucracy, the bizarre world of American voting, and the punishing aspects of personal finance like why checking your credit score can lower it, or why withdrawing your own money comes with so many fees.

Why do these odd things matter to us? Because they're part of our daily lives! They can make us wonder, laugh, or even get a little frustrated. But by understanding these weird bits, we can maybe start to think about how they could be made better.

Let's dive into these mysteries together and figure out what's really going on with all this weird stuff. Get ready to think hard as we look into these silly situations. So buckle up—it's time to learn and possibly even make some changes! Join me as we solve these strange puzzles. Who knows? Maybe along the way, we'll find ways to fix them.

Introduction

In the United States, we pride ourselves on being a land of opportunity. Yet, as we look closer, we see that opportunities are not equally available to everyone. Our systems—be they educational, political, or economic—often perpetuate inequalities rather than mitigate them. This book aims to confront these issues head-on, offering a deep dive into the policies that shape our daily lives.

Take education, for example. Imagine a child in a low-income neighborhood who is exceptionally bright but is limited by the poor quality of local schools. This child's potential is stifled not by a lack of ability, but by systemic barriers. Why should a zip code determine the quality of education a child receives? This question is just one of many that this book explores.

Another pressing issue is the influence of money in politics. Consider the case of a local election where the majority of campaign funds come from out-of-state donors. These contributions often reflect the interests of the donors rather than the constituents, skewing the democratic process. This book examines the implications of such practices and advocates for reforms that prioritize local voices.

Moreover, I address the challenges faced by working parents who struggle with the high cost of childcare. What if we could remove this financial burden and provide free, quality childcare for all families? Such a policy could transform lives, enabling parents to work and contribute to the economy without sacrificing their children's well-being.

These examples highlight the central theme of this book: there are many absurd policies that need to be reevaluated to create a better society. Each chapter presents a different aspect of this theme, offering examples and sometimes solutions as well. If you read the book to the end, I hope you will be inspired to advocate for policies that reflect a fairer society.

As you read, I encourage you to reflect on your own experiences and consider how these issues impact your life and the lives of those around you. Welcome to a world where common sense isn't so common and where every day puzzles await your curiosity. Let's dive in and see if we can make sense of the senseless.

Contents

ONE

CRIMINAL JUSTICE

CHAPTER 1

Why is an Accused Criminal Not Allowed to Speak Freely to Defend Himself While Accusers Can?

Imagine one day you find yourself accused of a crime you didn't commit. The charges are serious, and the potential consequences are life-changing. Naturally, you want to shout from the rooftops that you're innocent, to clear your name before your reputation is irreparably damaged. But then, you're hit with a gag order. This order legally prevents you from speaking publicly about your case. How would you feel?

Helpless? Frustrated?

What is a Gag Order?

A gag order is a directive issued by a court that restricts parties, witnesses, or attorneys from discussing certain aspects of a case publicly. It's arguably intended to protect the integrity of the legal process by preventing pretrial publicity from influencing potential jurors. Sounds reasonable at first, right? But here's where it gets contentious.

Isn't Free Speech Crucial for a Fair Trial?

In the United States, we pride ourselves on the rights to free speech and a fair trial, foundational pillars of our democracy. Yet, when a gag order clamps down on an accused person's ability to speak out, these two rights come into conflict. If you were gagged, unable to defend yourself in the court of public opinion where charges against you might be freely discussed by the media and prosecutors, would you feel like justice is being served?

The Unfair Advantage to Government

Consider the scenario where high-profile figures, like a former President or public official, are accused of a crime. The prosecution can make public comments and disclose details that frame the narrative, while the gag order muzzles the defense. The accused cannot counter misconceptions or defend their reputation, which shifts public perception and potentially pre-biases a jury. Is this disparity what our forefathers intended when they drafted the Constitution?

The Impact of Gag Orders

Gag orders don't just silence defendants. They also restrict what family, friends, and community members can say, isolating the accused at a time when support is most needed.

This sweeping silencing raises serious questions about the fairness and integrity of our justice system. How can we claim to uphold the right to a fair trial if we deny individuals the ability to openly defend themselves?

Is it Time for Change?

The use of gag orders needs a critical reexamination. For a justice system that claims to be fair and impartial, allowing those accused to speak freely is not just a matter of constitutional right—it's a cornerstone of genuine justice. If the essence of a fair trial is the ability to defend oneself against government allegations, then surely gag orders, which skew this balance, should be considered a threat to justice.

Rethinking Whether Gag Orders are Constitutional

Imagine you are gagged, your voice stifled, your side of the story unheard. This isn't just about legal principles—it's about protecting our fundamental human rights in the face of judicial proceedings. What would you do if you are not able to tell your side of the story while the government can talk day and night whether it's true or just made up lies? Do you think it's time the Supreme Court stepped in and declared gag orders unconstitutional, ensuring that every person has the right to defend themselves as guaranteed by the Constitution?

CHAPTER 2

Why Are US Citizen Criminals Stripped of Their Right to Vote?

You believe that smoking marijuana should be legal. You enjoy smoking, so you did. You are arrested and charged. Since you passionately believe that marijuana should be legal, you meet your local candidate for Congress who shares your belief. You want to vote for him. However, when you go to register to vote, you find out that you are not eligible. You wonder, how can you not be allowed to vote if you are a United States citizen? How would you feel? Betrayed? Silenced?

Citizens Have Right to Vote

The right to vote is a cornerstone of American democracy. It's how Americans express their will and affect change. When individuals are barred from voting because of a criminal record, it raises a critical question: Are these citizens not allowed to participate in democracy?

To understand how crazy this is, let's try another example. Imagine you are against slavery. You help a slave escape. Then you are charged for helping a slave escape. You become a criminal, so you cannot vote for a political candidate who can get rid of slavery. How will you be able to make change in an unjust system or change unjust laws?

Historical Context

The history of felon disenfranchisement laws in the United States reveals a troubling pattern. These laws were often instituted during times of racial and social strife, with the intent of disenfranchising minority groups and those in lower socio-economic classes. By stripping these individuals of their voting rights, the powerful could maintain control and suppress dissent. This historical context raises significant concerns about the fairness and motives behind such laws.

Right to Vote Comes With Citizenship

Even if a citizen commits a crime, they remain a citizen. Citizenship comes with inalienable rights, among which is the right to vote. Denying this right based on a past mistake contradicts the essence of citizenship. It suggests that some citizens are less deserving of their rights than others, which is antithetical to the core values of democracy where citizens choose to govern themselves.

A Tool for Political Manipulation

Imagine living in a society where the government can criminalize dissent and strip opponents of their voting rights. This scenario may seem far-fetched, but it highlights the potential for abuse inherent in disenfranchisement laws. By removing voting rights from those deemed criminals, the government gains a tool to silence opposition and maintain power. This dynamic is dangerous for any democracy, as it opens the door to tyranny and corruption.

Criminality is Not a Revocation of Citizenship

When someone commits a crime, they are sentenced to serve time or pay fines as retribution and rehabilitation. Once they've completed their sentence, society considers their debt paid. However, denying the right to vote extends a citizen's punishment indefinitely. Not only is this against democracy, but it also does not align with the ideals of rehabilitation and second chances. Instead, it perpetuates a cycle of exclusion and marginalization. Ensuring that every citizen, regardless of their past, has the right to vote is not just a matter of fairness—it's essential for the health and integrity of our democracy. Ensuring that all citizens are allowed to vote strengthens democracy and ensures a more representative and fair political process.

If you committed a crime as a teenager, do you think you should lose your voting rights? Do you think an individual who wanted to abolish slavery and was then convicted as a criminal should not be allowed to vote to eliminate slavery? Is it time for the United States to uphold its democratic ideals and restore voting rights to all its citizens, ensuring that our democracy truly represents the will of the people?

CHAPTER 3

Why Does the Government Publicly Announce the Indictment?

Imagine you wake up one morning to find your name splashed across the headlines of every major news outlet. The government has indicted you in a secret court without your knowledge. Before you even have a chance to grasp the situation, your friends, family, colleagues, and even strangers start viewing you as a criminal and stop talking to you regardless of whether the allegations against you are true. This is just the beginning of a long, arduous journey that, regardless of the outcome, will tarnish your reputation forever regardless of whether you are guilty or not.

Indictment Favors the Government

The government, with its massive resources, can accuse you of a crime for almost anything, and this accusation alone is irreparably damaging. You see, when the government indicts you, it doesn't need to prove that you are guilty. For them, it's just the first step in a long legal process that may be motivated by a number of reasons. But for you, the accused, the repercussions are immediate. If you are accused you have to defend yourself, spend a lot of money and time, and your reputation starts to suffer right away. The public often equates an indictment as guilt, which destroys your reputation and upends your life in the blink of an eye. You're now left with the enormous task of clearing your name, a battle fought on two fronts: in court, and in the court of public opinion.

Government prosecutors gain an unfair advantage by limiting a defendant's ability to speak publicly by imposing a gag order, especially in cases when prosecutors selectively leak information to the media before the defendant is arraigned. As a result, the defendant's reputation is already damaged, which unfairly prejudices in the eyes of the public.

As you scramble to defend yourself, hiring lawyers and managing spiraling legal fees, you realize how the scales are tipped. The government, with its vast resources, holds the upper hand. By indicting you, the government has effectively put you on trial to prove your innocence. This is the exact opposite of what the justice system is about. The government is supposed to prove beyond a reasonable doubt that you created a crime. By making your indictment public, the government wins without proving anything. Even if you are confident that the truth will prevail, the journey to clear your name is costly and draining.

Indictment Irreparably Damages Your Reputation No Matter Whether You are Guilty or Innocent

You might think that once you are found not guilty in a court, life will go back to normal. However, the stain of an indictment isn't easily washed away. People remember the accusations but often forget or ignore the outcome, especially if it's an acquittal.

You might think, "But I didn't do anything wrong, the truth will come out!" However, in the current system, the truth might not be enough. Prosecutors wield enormous power—they can decide whom to charge, what charges to bring, and even influence where the trial could take place. This isn't just about one bad day turning into a legal nightmare; it's about a systemic flaw that allows for unchecked prosecutorial discretion.

Imagine high-profile cases, like those of celebrities or public figures, where despite acquittals, their lives and careers remain forever altered under the shadow of their past indictment. There have been many public figures, celebrities, and even everyday people who were indicted, went through a trial, and were found not guilty. But by that time, the media had already painted a picture of them that was hard to change. Their lives were altered dramatically, with some losing their jobs, friends, and facing public anger. Do you remember OJ Simpson, Kyle Rittenhouse, Kaycee Anthony or many people found by the Innocence Project who served on death row for years before they were found innocent? Their and their family's reputation and life never reversed back to normal.

Now, think about how this would feel for you, trying to return to your normal life, facing neighbors, job prospects, and social settings knowing people will still hold doubts about your innocence. News spreads fast, and people often remember the accusation but forget the outcome. So, even if you are found not guilty, the damage to your reputation lasts forever.

The Deep Bias of Selective Prosecution

Consider how this power could be misused. A prosecutor could target someone based on biased views, personal vendettas, or even political pressure. Imagine they decide you're an easy target or a means to an end in their career. Your life could be turned upside down because someone with power saw an opportunity, not because you did anything to deserve it.

Venue Shopping: Stacking the Deck

Adding to the complexity, imagine that the prosecutor can choose a venue they know will favor their side, not a neutral setting that ensures a fair trial. This isn't just a theoretical risk—it happens, and it can significantly affect the outcome of your case.

Should There be Consequences for the Government if it Unfairly Accused a Person Who was In Fact Innocent?

History is full of cases where the government maliciously put an innocent person on trial. You just need to see the examples in the south. A Black man fell in love with a White woman. The White prosecutor, sheriff, judge and jury made sure the man got the maximum sentence in prison. In many cases, the man was accused of murder and sentenced to death.

Being indicted isn't just about dealing with the legal case; it's about handling the court of public opinion too. Many people who are acquitted still struggle to rebuild their lives because the shadow of the indictment lingers.

Absolute Immunity: A Double-Edged Sword

Now, let's say the charges are baseless and the case against you is weak or even fabricated. You might think that after you are found innocent in a court, you could seek justice against the prosecutor for their negligence or malice. Unfortunately, in America, prosecutors have what's called "absolute immunity." This means they can't be held legally accountable for most actions taken while they're performing their prosecutorial duties, no matter how wrongful those actions might be.

As you reflect on this scenario, consider the broader implications. Shouldn't there be consequences for the government if it maliciously accuses someone who is, in fact, innocent? How can we ensure that individuals are not only given a fair trial but also protected from the life-altering impact of a public indictment? What do you think we can do to ensure that people's reputations aren't destroyed unfairly? Should there be more protection for the accused? Should the government be immune or should the government be held responsible for destroying the life of innocent people? Should the government lose immunity and the government be allowed to be sued in both personal and professional capacities? What is a fairer way to create a fair justice system that not only punishes criminals but emphasizes on protecting the innocent people?

CHAPTER 4

Why is the Government Allowed to Make Plea Deals with Accused Criminals?

Imagine you are Rachel, a single mom living in a small Missouri town, struggling to make ends meet while raising two young children. One evening, while you're at a local grocery store, a misunderstanding leads to your arrest on charges of shoplifting—a crime you did not commit. You're taken into police custody. You are confused and worried about who will take care of your kids while you're detained.

In the interrogation room, the government prosecutor presents you with a stark choice: plead guilty to a lesser charge of petty theft, or face the possibility of a felony charge and potentially years in prison if you decide to fight the charges. Despite your innocence, the threat of losing your children and your inability to afford a competent attorney weigh heavily on you. The prosecutor's words echo in your mind, "This is your best option. It'll all go away, and you can go back to your kids soon."

Scared and feeling cornered, you accept the plea deal. You're fined, and a criminal record is added to your good name, all for a crime you never committed. This plea not only impacts your immediate situation but also your future opportunities and your family's reputation, casting a long shadow over your life and your children's lives.

The Unfair Reality of Plea Deals

Rachel's story is not unique in the American criminal justice system. For many, especially the poor, plea deals are not a choice but a coercion, a forced compromise dictated by a fear of harsher penalties and an inability to fight a prolonged legal battle. This chapter explores why a system seemingly designed for efficiency and expediency fails to deliver justice for the most vulnerable.

In the criminal justice system, a plea deal is like a shortcut. It's when you are accused of a crime agree to say you're guilty in exchange for a lighter punishment. This system is really unfair for innocent poor people who didn't do anything wrong. Why? Because they don't have money to hire an attorney to defend themselves. Also, since the government can make up crimes for almost anything, poor people are almost resource-less to fight so they take a deal.

Who Takes Plea Deals?

Research has consistently shown that racial minorities and those from lower socioeconomic backgrounds are more likely to be offered and accept plea deals involving jail time. These groups often don't have the money for a strong defense, so they're more likely to take a plea deal, even if they're innocent. This can lead to more people from these groups ending up with criminal records, which isn't fair.

Why is this a Problem?

Plea deals can be especially tough on people who don't have much money or who can't afford a good lawyer. These people might feel like they can't fight the charges against them, so they take the deal. But this means they end up with a criminal record for something they didn't do. It's like being punished for being poor.

A vast majority of criminal cases in the United States never go to trial. It's estimated that about 90% to 95% of both federal and state cases end in plea deals. This means only a small fraction of cases are decided by a judge or jury in a courtroom.

Pressure and Injustice

1. **Coercion Over Choice:** For many, accepting a plea deal isn't a real choice. It's a response to pressure and fear. The threat of facing a much harsher sentence if found guilty at trial pushes many to accept guilt even when they are innocent.

2. **Impact on Future Opportunities:** A guilty plea, even as part of a deal, can have long-term consequences. It can affect job prospects, housing opportunities, and even the right to vote. This is a heavy price to pay, especially for those who are innocent.

Constitutional Rights in Question

The Sixth Amendment of the U.S. Constitution guarantees the right to a fair and speedy trial. However, the widespread use of plea deals undermines this right, as many defendants waive their right to a trial in fear of harsher punishment.

Given these issues, the argument for declaring plea deals unconstitutional becomes stronger:

- **Right to a Fair Trial:** The overwhelming use of plea deals can be seen as a circumvention of the constitutional right to a fair trial.
- **Equal Protection Under the Law:** The disparities in who is offered and who accepts plea deals suggest a violation of the principle of equal protection under the law.

Do Poor People Get Fairness and Equality in Sentencing?

In a fair system, everyone should get the exact same sentence for the same crime, not a sentence that changes because of a plea deal.

Imagine a world where plea deals don't exist and every person accused of a crime gets a fair chance in court where the burden is on the government to prove the guilt beyond a reasonable doubt. Do you think this would make our justice system fairer? How should we address the challenges of ensuring that everyone, regardless of income or race, receives equal treatment under the law?

What do you think of banning the system of plea deals?

- Why not allow every defendant an opportunity for a fair trial?
- Why not make the justice system more transparent, with decisions based on evidence, not negotiations or scare tactics behind closed doors?
- Will abolishing plea deals force the system to deal only with cases it can handle, possibly leading to less punitive and more rehabilitative approaches?

CHAPTER 5

Why Can't You Get Automatic Grant of Change of Venue Request?

What Does 'Transferring Venue Mean?

Transferring a venue means moving a trial to a different location. It sounds simple, but it's a complex issue deeply tied to fairness in the legal process. Why would someone want to transfer their trial venue? Often, it's because the original location is prejudicial, or logistically problematic, which could hinder a fair defense.

Location Disadvantages You But Not the Government

You, as the accused, are fighting not just the charges against you, but also the logistical and emotional burdens of being far from home. The government, on the other hand, has resources everywhere. Since the laws of the State are the same regardless of where you live in the State and where the crime was committed, the government can prosecute the case anywhere in that State. Similarly, if you are facing a Federal charge, the case can easily be moved to anywhere in the country since the Federal laws are the same in the country. Also, the Federal government prosecutors and courts are everywhere in the country.

Why Venue Matters for the Defendant?

In an ideal justice system, every part of the trial process, including the location, is geared toward ensuring fairness. That includes giving the defendant—a real person with rights—a say in where the trial should be held. But often, this isn't the case. The decision tends to be skewed towards what's convenient for the prosecution, not what's fair.

You're up against the full power of the government when you're on trial. That's intimidating enough without the added stress of an unfriendly venue. Here's why the place matters:

- **Fair and Impartial Trial:** Local prejudices or preconceived notions can deeply impact jury impartiality. A neutral venue can help ensure jurors who are unbiased and fair.
- **Access to Resources:** Being close to your legal team, having access to personal documents, or simply being able to sleep in your own bed can make a significant difference in your capacity to mount a strong defense.
- **Reducing Bias:** In smaller or tight-knit communities, the court of public opinion can heavily influence the

actual court. Changing the venue can mitigate this and protect the judicial process.

The Need for Flexibility in Venue Choices

Think about fairness for a moment. If you're trying to defend yourself in a place that's inherently biased or unfamiliar, your odds of receiving a fair trial are nearly impossible. Shouldn't you have the right to argue your case in a place that doesn't disadvantage you? Where the jurors can understand the context of your life and background? Allowing more flexibility in choosing the venue could help balance the scales of justice, making the legal process fairer, especially for those without extensive resources.

Your Perspective on Justice

For justice to be truly just, it must be accessible and fair on all fronts, including where a trial is held. Advocating for more defendant-friendly venue laws isn't just about logistics; it's about protecting the fundamental rights of every person who enters the courtroom. Wouldn't you want the power to move your trial to a more neutral location? What does fairness in the justice system mean to you, and how important is the setting in achieving that fairness?

CHAPTER 6

Why Does America Love Filling Prisons?

Did you know that the United States has one of the highest numbers of people in prison in the world? It's a surprising fact, but it's true. Many of these people are in jail for non-violent crimes, which means they didn't hurt anyone physically. This brings us to a big question: Does it really make sense to put so many non-violent people behind bars?

Why So Many People Are in Prison

There are laws in America that are really strict about certain offenses, even if they're not violent. Things like inability to pay fines, stealing something, using illegal drugs, or even writing a bad check can land someone in jail. Because of these laws, prisons are filled with people who haven't hurt anyone.

The Cost of Keeping Non-Violent People in Prison

Running prisons is expensive. It costs the government, and therefore taxpayers like you a lot of money. Housing, feeding, and taking care of the health needs of prisoners add up to billions of dollars every year. And when non-violent people are locked up, they can't work, take care of their families, or contribute to society.

The Impact on Families and Communities

When someone is sent to prison, it's not just hard on them. It's tough on their families and communities too. Kids are forced to grow up without a parent, and families can struggle financially. Communities also suffer when too many of its members are locked away.

The focus on punishment over rehabilitation has resulted in high recidivism rates, where former inmates return to prison due to lack of support for reintegration into society.

Prisons Are Failing in their Intended Objectives

Perhaps the government created many laws that enabled the mass prison population. If their intent was that prisons will serve as a deterrence to committing crime, that has not worked. A significant number of released prisoners are rearrested within a few years of release. The high rate of recidivism in the United States points to the ineffectiveness of the prison system as a rehabilitative institution.

Need for Prison Reform

- **Civil Actions:** Instead of putting people in jail, the government can try civil actions such as reasonable fines, community services, or mandatory volunteering opportunities.
- **Focus on Rehabilitation:** Shift the focus of prisons from punishment to rehabilitation, including more robust mental health services, educational programs, and vocational training to prepare inmates for post-release life.
- **Restorative Justice Programs:** Implement restorative justice programs that involve mediation and reconciliation with victims, which have been shown to significantly reduce recidivism rates.
- **Community-based Sentencing:** For non-violent offenders, explore alternatives to incarceration such as community service which are less costly and can be more effective at rehabilitation.

Impact of Reform

Prison reform can lead to:

- Decreased prison populations and lower costs for taxpayers.
- Reduced recidivism rates through better preparation for reintegration.
- A more humane and just penal system that helps individuals become productive members of society.

Is Prison the Right Answer to All Issues?

Imagine if someone stole something because they were really in need. How about a kid who took a Coke from McDonald's and didn't pay? Do you think six months in prison is the best option for the kid? What about someone who made a mistake but regrets his actions and wants to do better? How about thinking of the deeper question of why we failed as a society in producing people who would not pay for the Coke?

CHAPTER 7

What's the Rationale for Putting Non-Violent Criminals in Prison?

Imagine you have a neighbor named Dave. He's always been a quiet, law-abiding citizen, involved in community events, and never misses a neighborhood barbecue. One day, you learn that Dave has been arrested for tax evasion. He made some errors on his tax returns—not out of greed, but out of ignorance and confusion with the overly complex tax laws. Now, Dave faces the possibility of spending years in prison.

You might wonder, "Why should Dave go to prison for this? Isn't there a better way to handle his mistake?" This situation brings us to a critical question: what's the rationale for putting non-violent criminals like Dave in prison?

The Historical Context of Prisons

Originally, prisons were built to detain individuals who posed a direct physical threat to society—people who committed violent crimes. The goal was clear: keep dangerous individuals away from the public to maintain safety. Those people, if remained free, were highly likely to cause a loss of life. However, as you see in Dave's case, the modern use of incarceration has strayed far from these original intentions.

The Evolution of Crime and Punishment

Over the centuries, what we consider a crime has dramatically expanded. Today, non-violent offenses, including financial missteps like Dave's, can lead to severe punitive measures. This shift reflects changes in our societal and economic structures but raises crucial questions about the appropriate use of incarceration.

Why Rethink Incarceration for Non-Violent Crimes?

Incarcerating non-violent offenders often does little to deter crime or rectify the harm caused. Instead, it leads to overcrowded prisons and drains public resources, all while doing nothing to compensate victims or rehabilitate the offender. For people like Dave, prison won't educate him about tax laws or repay the taxes he owes. There must be a better way.

Ineffectiveness of Current Punitive Measures

In contemporary society, white-collar crimes, such as fraud or embezzlement, and non-compliance offenses can lead to lengthy prison sentences. The punitive approach often fails to compensate victims while costing taxpayers significantly through expensive, prolonged legal processes and incarceration. The imprisonment of non-violent offenders, particularly those involved in complex financial crimes, often does little to deter crime or rectify the harm caused to victims. You can look at some very controversial figures for example:

- **Jeffrey Skilling (Enron CEO)**: His actions or inactions contributed to the collapse of Enron. Thousands of employees lost their jobs. Thousands of investors lost their savings.
- **Sam Bankman-Fried (FTX Founder)**: The collapse of FTX caused billions of dollars of loss for investors and customers.

While both Skilling and Bankman-Friend were prosecuted by the government, these cases also open a good discussion. As we read earlier, prison has not been a deterrence. Hence, we see new cases. Then the question is what happens to the victims. How did the government's action of putting them in prison help the investors or customers who lost the money? Will they get their money back? In these cases, the measure of success has been "lengthy sentences". But those lengthy sentences will not bring the money back. Incarceration satisfies the government's punitive urge but is unlikely to the victims.

Instead of the government focusing on punishing the accused, how about shifting the focus to helping the victims?

Alternative Approaches to Non-Violent Crime

Rather than sending Dave to prison on in the above example of Skilling and Bankman-Fried, imagine if we focus on restitution and rehabilitation:

- **Restitution and Financial Penalties:** Instead of traditional incarceration, require offenders to return the stolen funds with substantial penalties. For instance, mandating the return of embezzled funds with a tenfold penalty could provide direct compensation to victims and serve as a strong deterrent. In this case, Dave, Skilling, Bankman-Fried could be required to pay back the owed taxes along with a significant fine. This approach directly addresses the wrongdoing and compensates for the evasion without removing the accused criminals from society.
- **Economic Contribution in Lieu of Incarceration:** Enforce a system where convicted white-collar criminals must work, but their income (beyond a basic living wage) is directed towards compensating their victims. This approach not only ensures ongoing contribution back to society but also helps inculcate a sense of responsibility and restitution in the offender. Suppose Dave, Skilling, or Bankman-Fried could continue working, but a portion of their income is garnished to repay his debt to society. This method

ensures they contribute positively without the negative impacts of incarceration.

- **Tailored Rehabilitation Programs:** Implement programs designed to address the underlying motives of white-collar crimes, such as greed, addiction to risk, or ethical disengagement. These programs could focus on psychological counseling, ethical retraining, and skills development to better integrate offenders back into society as constructive individuals. Educational programs about tax law and financial management could prevent future offenses, helping Dave and others understand and comply with the law more effectively.

Advantages of Reforming Punitive Measures

1. **Victim Compensation:** Direct restitution to victims can alleviate some of the financial damages and personal anguish caused by these crimes.
2. **Reduction in Incarceration Costs:** Shifting from incarceration to alternative punishment for non-violent crimes can significantly reduce the financial burden on the state.
3. **Societal Benefits:** Encouraging offenders to contribute economically can transform a punitive system into one that promotes positive social contributions.

Civilian Approach Instead of Criminal Approach

As we reflect on Dave's situation and the broader use of prisons for non-violent crimes, it's clear that a shift in how we administer justice is necessary. By focusing on rehabilitation and restitution rather than retribution, we can achieve a more just and practical approach to handling non-violent offenses. Imagine being part of this reformative movement. How would you change the system to ensure fair treatment for non-violent offenders like Dave? What ideas do you have that could transform our approach to justice?

CHAPTER 8

Does Putting People Behind Bars for a Long Time Help America?

Let's say you're a young adult caught with a small amount of illegal drugs. Instead of rehabilitation or a second chance, you're handed a decade-long sentence. Inside, instead of learning how to avoid drugs or improve your life skills, you're often learning how to survive in a harsh environment. By the time you're released, your employment prospects are bleak, your social skills are rusty, and you're viewed permanently through the lens of your past mistakes.

The criminal justice system often resorts to long sentences as a deterrent against crimes, from minor drug offenses to severe acts of violence like murder or rape. While the intent is to protect society by keeping dangerous individuals away for extended periods, the actual effects of such policies may be contrary to the desired outcomes.

The Psychology Behind Long Sentences

Long-term imprisonment is predicated on the assumption that extended isolation from society prevents crime and reforms offenders. However, since the evolution, humans have largely developed behaviors based on their environments:

- **Environmental Influence:** Prisons, often being violent and oppressive, are more likely to cultivate aggression and desperation rather than rehabilitation.
- **Identity Transformation:** Extended exposure to the criminal elements within prisons can lead individuals to adopt criminal identities, making them more likely to reoffend upon release.

Are Long Sentences Doing More Harm Than Good?

Long sentences are supposed to deter crime and protect society, right? But what if they're doing more harm than good, especially for non-violent offenders? Think about it:

- **Social and Psychological Effects:** Being incarcerated for lengthy periods for non-violent crimes can lead to unnecessary social isolation, mental health issues, and increased hostility towards societal norms. It's tough to maintain relationships or develop new ones when you're isolated.

- **Criminal Skill Development:** Prisons may serve as universities of crime where non-violent offenders learn criminal skills from hardened inmates, increasing the likelihood of serious criminal behavior in the future.
- **Economic Impact:** It's not just costly for you; it's expensive for everyone. Keeping someone in prison costs a lot of money—money that could potentially be used for more effective programs that help people rebuild their lives.

Reconsidering Long Sentences

What if, instead of locking you away for years, the system focused on what led you to commit the crime in the first place? What if the justice system prioritized rehabilitation over punishment, education over isolation, and restoration over retribution?

- **Proportional Sentencing:** Imagine if sentences were tailored not just to the crime, but also to the individual's circumstances, focusing on integrating rather than segregating them from society.
- **Rehabilitative Measures:** What about replacing long jail terms with programs designed to address personal issues like drug addiction, providing education, or teaching job skills?
- **Restorative Justice:** Consider a system where you, as an offender, have the opportunity to understand the impact of your actions, make amends, and be reintegrated into your community.

Building a Better Society

To truly enhance societal safety and health, it is crucial to reconsider the reliance on long sentences. A shift towards rehabilitation, proportional sentencing, and restorative justice not only aligns with humane principles but is also supported by evidence suggesting these methods are more effective at reducing recidivism and aiding societal integration. As society evolves, so too must our approaches to criminal justice, emphasizing healing and correction over retribution and isolation. Imagine you have the power to reshape how we think about and implement justice, especially for non-violent crimes. How would you redesign the system? What steps would you take to ensure that when people serve their time, they return to society not only ready but able to contribute positively?

CHAPTER 9

Why is Every Little Thing a Crime?

In many jurisdictions, the legal system is burdened with laws that criminalize minor behaviors, creating penalties that often do not proportionately match the actions. This chapter argues for a critical reassessment of what behaviors warrant criminal penalties and advocates for the decriminalization of minor offenses.

The Spectrum of Criminal Laws

Laws are intended to maintain order and protect citizens, but when they are misapplied, they can cause more harm than good. Many acts currently punishable by law are disproportionately penalized, reflecting outdated legislative thinking rather than a measured response to the behavior.

Examples of Disproportionate Legal Penalties

- **Jaywalking:** In many cities, pedestrians can be fined heavily for crossing the street against a traffic signal, even when no traffic is present. In extreme cases, repeated offenses could lead to arrest or imprisonment.
- **Loitering:** Laws against loitering can be used to target specific populations, including the homeless and minorities, leading to unnecessary interactions with the criminal justice system.
- **Truancy:** Teenagers skipping school can lead to their parents being fined or imprisoned in some states, a punishment that may exacerbate family hardships.
- **Drug Possession:** The possession of small amounts of controlled substances can lead to long prison sentences, significantly impacting lives and contributing to an overloaded prison system.

The Social and Economic Costs

The costs of criminalizing minor offenses are significant:

- **Financial Burden:** Enforcement, court proceedings, and incarceration for minor offenses cost taxpayers billions annually.
- **Social Impact:** Minor infractions can result in a criminal record, which affects one's ability to find employment, secure housing, and access educational opportunities.

- **Community Relations:** Over-policing for minor crimes can lead to distrust and resentment towards law enforcement within communities.

Government Motivations and Misguided Policies

There is a growing concern that some criminal laws are more about generating revenue through fines and fees or controlling certain populations than about maintaining public safety. This misalignment of priorities suggests the need for a thorough review and rationalization of the penal code.

Decriminalization

To address these issues, several steps can be recommended:

1. **Reevaluate Minor Offenses:** Laws should be critically reviewed to determine if they still serve the public interest.
2. **Implement Proportional Penalties:** Penalties should be proportional to the offense's actual societal impact. This approach can prevent the legal system from disproportionately damaging individuals' lives over minor infractions.
3. **Promote Civil Penalties Over Criminal Ones:** Where appropriate, replace criminal penalties with civil penalties or community service, which do not result in criminal records.
4. **Focus on Rehabilitation and Education:** For behaviors that stem from social issues, focus on

providing supportive services, rehabilitation, or educational programs rather than punitive measures.

Toward a Rational and Fair Legal System

The principle that the punishment should fit the crime is fundamental to justice. As society progresses, so too must our laws and their applications. Decriminalizing minor offenses and rationalizing the legal system to focus on genuine threats to public safety can lead to better social outcomes, reduce unnecessary expenditures, and rebuild trust in the legal system. Consider your local laws: Are there minor behaviors criminalized that do not threaten public safety? How would you propose reforming these laws to create a fairer, more rational legal system?

CHAPTER 10

What's Up with Mandatory Minimum Sentences for Minor Offenses?

You are driving home one night, and without realizing it, you fail to fully stop at a stop sign. An officer pulls you over, and upon searching your vehicle—perhaps without much cause—finds a small amount of a controlled substance in the glove compartment, left there by a friend without your knowledge. Suddenly, you're not just looking at a traffic ticket; you're facing a mandatory minimum sentence for drug possession. This isn't just a hypothetical scenario—it's a reality for many, and it could happen to you.

The Problem with Mandatory Minimums

Mandatory minimum sentences were supposed to make justice more uniform. No more lenient sentences for the wealthy and harsh ones for the poor, right? But here's what really happens: These laws strip judges of the ability to tailor sentences to the circumstances of a case. Everyone gets the same harsh penalty, no matter the details. What if the judge believes your story and thinks rehabilitation or probation is more appropriate? Too bad. Their hands are tied.

Disproportionate Punishments

Think about it: How does it make sense that you, caught with a tiny amount of a controlled substance by accident, could end up with the same prison sentence as someone who intentionally breaks the law? These punishments aren't just harsh; they're often wildly out of proportion to the crime.

The Human Cost

Now, let's consider the bigger picture. You're in prison for several years. What happens to your job? Your apartment? Your family? The effects ripple out, disrupting not just your life but also those of your loved ones. Kids grow up without a parent, partners struggle with lost income, and when you finally get out, you're thrust back into a world where you no longer fit.

Removing Judicial Discretion

Under mandatory minimums, judges can't use their judgment. They're forced to apply these one-size-fits-all penalties, even when they believe a lighter sentence, like community service or probation, would be more appropriate and beneficial for everyone involved.

Increased Incarceration Rates

The United States has one of the highest incarceration rates in the world, and mandatory minimums are a big reason why. Prisons are overflowing with people who perhaps shouldn't even be there—people who made a small mistake and got caught in a legal sledgehammer.

What's the Alternative?

Imagine a system where judges have the power to look at each case individually. Instead of sending you straight to prison, they could evaluate the specifics—your intent, your history, the amount of substance—and decide on a punishment that actually fits the crime. More flexibility could mean more justice.

Time for Change

Mandatory minimum sentences, especially for non-violent and minor offenses, represent a critical failure in the justice system. Originally intended to ensure uniformity and deterrence, they often lead to unjust outcomes and overcrowded prisons. It's time we rethink mandatory minimums, especially for non-violent offenses. Justice isn't just about punishing; it's about finding the right response to each unique situation. If you were in that situation, caught at the wrong place at the wrong time, wouldn't you want a judge to have the freedom to use their discretion?

CHAPTER 11

How About Decriminalizing Poverty?

You're juggling two jobs just to keep the roof over your head and food on the table. It's tough but manageable—until one day, you get slapped with a $100 parking ticket. Might not sound like a lot, but for you, it's a choice between emptying your bank account and going hungry. You decide to feed your family instead of paying the fine right away. But the costs don't stop there; they start snowballing, and now you're facing even bigger penalties.

The criminalization of poverty is a systemic issue where minor legal infractions disproportionately affect the poor. This practice perpetuates a cycle of poverty and legal entanglement that can have devastating long-term effects on individuals and communities alike.

The Brutal Cycle of Poverty and Punishment

You're not alone in this. The system seems rigged against those struggling financially. Here's how it hits you hard:

When Fines Become Mountains

Let's say the ticket costs $100—a big chunk of your weekly income. You have to make a choice: pay the ticket or pay for essentials like groceries or your child's medication. You choose the essentials, of course. But then, the fine increases because it's late, and eventually, you could even face having your car towed or your license suspended over this one unpaid ticket. Now, how do you get to work? How do you take your kids to school?

The Trap of the Bail System

Imagine another scenario: You're arrested for a minor offense—maybe something as small as jaywalking in the wrong place at the wrong time. You're taken to jail, and bail is set at $500. For you, it's unaffordable. Unable to pay, you end up stuck in jail, perhaps losing your job in the process, which only deepens your financial crisis. You being poor made you a criminal.

The Domino Effect of Legal Financial Struggles

Consider what happens with continual penalties for small offenses like a public transportation fare evasion. Imagine you are a young adult from a poor family who is fined for $20 fare evasion on public transit. The fine, compounded by additional administrative fees, quickly becomes unmanageable. With no resources to pay, you face jail time, creating a criminal record that will significantly hinder future employment opportunities.

Non-violent and minor offenses, such as traffic violations or public disturbance, can lead to fines that, if unpaid, accumulate additional fees or even convert into jail time. For those already struggling financially, this can result in an inescapable debt cycle.

Now imagine you are a single parent driving around in the morning to drop off your kids at two different schools. You are running late for your work. You are pulled over and you get a speeding ticket. Unable to pay the ticket due to immediate financial obligations (rent, childcare, etc.), the fines increase due to non-payment, and your license is eventually suspended. Unable to drive, you lose one of your jobs, deepening your financial distress.

Many states suspend drivers' licenses for unpaid fines and fees, regardless of the offense's nature. This policy disproportionately affects the poor, removing their ability to legally drive, often a necessity. You might think, "It's just a suspended license; I can manage." But think about how essential driving is for your daily responsibilities. Losing your license means potentially losing your job, your ability to care for your family, and your independence.

Every added fee makes it harder to climb out of poverty. The system is supposed to maintain order, but does it have to ruin lives to do so?

Isn't There a Better Way?

What if we stopped punishing poverty with more poverty? What if fines were based on what you could actually afford, or if community service was an option instead of jail time?

Examples That Could Change Lives

- **Ending Cash Bail for Non-Violent Offenses:** Why not assess someone's risk instead of their bank account? Replace cash bail with more equitable measures that assess individual risk rather than financial capability. Implementing risk assessments can prevent unnecessary detention for those not deemed a flight risk or a danger to the community.
- **Halting License Suspensions for Unpaid Fines:** Isn't it counterproductive to take away someone's ability to earn a living over unpaid debts? Why not prohibit the suspension of drivers' licenses for non-payment of fines unrelated to driving offenses? This policy change would prevent a cascade of consequences stemming from the inability to legally drive.

The Benefits Are Clear

By decriminalizing poverty, we not only reduce jail overcrowding but also support the economic stability of families. Eliminating criminalization of poverty offers multiple benefits:

- **Reduced Overcrowding in Jails:** By eliminating cash bail and not incarcerating people for unpaid fines, jails are less likely to be overcrowded with those who have committed minor infractions.
- **Economic Stability for Vulnerable Populations:** Ensuring that penalties do not disproportionately affect the poor helps maintain the economic stability of vulnerable populations, fostering healthier communities.
- **Long-Term Cost Savings:** Reducing the number of people in jail for minor offenses can lead to significant savings in public funds, which can be redirected towards more effective community services.

Could This Be You?

Imagine you don't have a fat bank account; would you think in a different way? What if the next ticket, the next fine, lands you in this cycle? How would you manage? Isn't it time for a change that stops criminalizing you for being unable to pay? Decriminalizing poverty isn't just about being lenient; it's about being logical and building a better society. It involves understanding and addressing the ways in which legal and economic systems entrenched disadvantage. It's about stopping a harmful cycle that takes a toll not just on individuals, but on entire society. It's about creating a justice system that truly aims to help people, not just penalize. Such reforms not only uphold the principles of fairness but also promote social stability and nation's well-being.

CHAPTER 12

How About Thinking of a Victim's Perspective Rather than the Government's?

Imagine you're taking a stroll through your neighborhood one evening. Suddenly, you find yourself in a heated argument with your neighbor, Jake. Tempers flare, and in a moment of anger, you punch him. Another neighbor calls the police. Now, Jake has known you for years. He knows this isn't typical behavior for you; you're generally a good person who just made a bad choice. You apologize sincerely, and he forgives you. However, the situation doesn't end there.

The government's prosecutor steps in with the power to drastically alter your life. Despite Jake's forgiveness, the prosecutor decides to press charges, aiming for the harshest penalties possible. This approach doesn't consider Jake's wishes or your momentary lapse—it only seeks punishment.

Empowering Victims and Rebalancing Justice

What if our system were different? What if, instead of prosecutors holding all the cards, victims like Jake could decide how to resolve the situation? Imagine a system where victims can choose to settle the matter through mediation or restorative justice, rather than being forced into a grueling, punitive trial at the expense of the government.

Expanding the Role of Victims in the Justice System

Currently, our system often sidelines victims, treating the state as the primary aggrieved party. This overlooks the direct impact on actual victims—real people whose lives are disrupted by these incidents. But what if Jake could decide what he feels is just?

Victim's Choice in Prosecution

Let's say Jake decides that, because of your apology and your history, he doesn't want you to face severe legal repercussions. He prefers a resolution that fosters understanding and reconciliation, not one that ruins your life. Jake's decision would play a crucial role. If he chooses to settle, the prosecutor's role would shift to facilitating that settlement, acting more as a mediator than an adversary.

Role of Prosecutors as Investigators and Mediators

Prosecutors would focus on gathering facts and facilitating dialogue between you and Jake, helping to reach an amicable settlement if both parties are willing. They would ensure that any agreement is fair and voluntary, safeguarding the interests of both the victim and the accused.

Public Trials as a Last Resort

If a settlement isn't feasible, either because of the crime's nature or because one party isn't interested in compromising, then the case might proceed to trial. This would ensure that the option for a public, transparent judicial process remains available, preserving the integrity of our justice system.

Benefits of a Victim-Centric Approach

- **Enhances Fairness:** By involving victims directly in the justice process, we make the system more equitable, providing satisfaction to victims while avoiding unnecessary punitive measures.
- **Reduces Prosecutorial Bias:** Involving victims and neutral mediators can reduce the chances of biased decisions driven by prosecutorial discretion.
- **Restores Public Trust:** A transparent and fair process, with better outcomes for victims, will help rebuild faith in the criminal justice system.

Victim Centered Criminal Justice System

By centering the system around the needs and decisions of victims, while carefully balancing the rights of the accused, we can take significant steps toward a more just, equitable, and trusted legal system. Imagine if you were the victim, what would you do? Would you like to have control? Or would you like the government to use the incident to advance whatever they decide to do?

TWO

PUNITIVE FINANCE

CHAPTER 13

Is the Federal Government's Easy Student Loan Driving University Fees Higher?

You graduated from high school and went to a college of your choice. Like many of your friends, you took a federal student loan to cover the cost of college attendance. A few years after you finished college and went to work, you realized that college was too expensive. A huge chunk of your paycheck goes towards paying off your student loans. Then you wonder whether the ease with which you and millions of other students could obtain federal student loans has an unintended side effect.

The Catch with Easy Loans

If any student, regardless of what university of major she chooses, can easily borrow money to pay for college, what's stopping universities from raising their tuition fees? Imagine being a university administrator. You know that the students can borrow whatever it costs to attend your institution. With the federal government's easy money lending, there might be little incentive to keep tuition affordable. Why not charge more if the government is essentially guaranteeing the funds through student loans?

What if Loans Were Harder to Get?

What if the government made it tougher to secure these loans? Would universities still feel empowered to hike their fees if fewer students could afford to enroll without financial aid? This situation forces us to ask: Are easy loans really helping students, or are they just allowing universities to inflate their prices without improving the quality of education? What's truly beneficial for students like you in the long run?

The Burden of Big Loans

Imagine you're about to enroll in college or maybe you're already there, grappling with these loans. How would you feel about the possibility that your debt could dictate your financial well-being for decades? It's a tough situation that many graduates face, making it harder to save for a house, invest in retirement, or even afford day-to-day expenses. Education debt could follow you into your 40s, 50s, or even later.

While easy access to loans makes higher education attainable, it also contributes to the cycle of rising tuition fees and crippling debt. A balanced approach, where loans are accessible but come with stricter conditions, might push universities to maintain reasonable tuition fees, ensuring that students get a quality education without being saddled with lifelong debt. Do you think the ease of getting student loans has helped or hindered your financial stability? Could a reformed system better serve future students, ensuring they receive a valuable education without the heavy burden of debt?

CHAPTER 14

Why is College Tuition Not Tied To How Much Their Graduates Earn in Median Salary?

Imagine you've just graduated with a degree you're passionate about. You're ready to start your career and make a difference in the world. But there's a catch—you are starting your journey saddled with a massive amount of student loan debt, a burden you took on because you believed in the promise of a good education leading to a well-paying job.

Your Dilemma

You studied in a field you loved, encouraged by everyone around you that following your passion would lead to a fulfilling and profitable career. However, after graduation, you face a stark reality. The jobs available in your field don't pay nearly enough to cover your monthly loan payments, let alone allow you to live comfortably. The gap between what you owe and what you earn is not just a gap; it's a chasm.

Why Did It Happen?

Your university, like many others, raised its tuition fees every year. They did this knowing students like you could borrow the money through federal student loans to pay for it. The system was supposed to be a win-win: universities get their fees, and students get their education. But as you discovered, the scale is far from balanced.

The Burden of Large Loans

You find yourself deferring your dreams of buying a home or investing in your future because your student loan payments eat up most of your modest paycheck. You feel trapped, realizing that your education may not have been the investment you were told it would be. Instead, it's a financial anchor, pulling you down.

Aligning Tuition with Earnings

What if your tuition had been capped based on the typical earnings of graduates in your field? Imagine a system where no student's tuition could exceed the median first-year salary expected for their profession. If your expected median salary was $40,000, then your total tuition cost would also be $40,000—no more.

Benefits of This Approach

This change would have given you and your peers a fighting chance to manage your debts and build your lives without the disproportionate burden of student loans. Colleges would need to ensure their programs are affordable and justify their costs based on real-world earnings outcomes.

Impact on Educational Institutions

Schools might be prompted to adjust their tuition or redesign programs that don't offer a solid return on investment. This could foster a more responsible education system, where program costs are directly tied to the economic value they provide to graduates.

Your Reflection as a Potential Student

Higher education must not only be accessible but also economically sensible. Tying tuition to graduate earnings isn't just about affordability; it's about fairness and ensuring that students like you can invest in your education without risking financial ruin.

Imagine you are about to choose a college or a major. Knowing what happens if you graduate with a heavy loan, how would this influence your decision? Would a tuition cap tied to potential earnings change how you think about the value of your education?

CHAPTER 15

Why are Student Loan Interest Rates So High?

You remember the excitement of graduating from college, degree in hand, ready to embark on your career journey. But as you enter the working world, you quickly realize that the student loan you took out to finance your education has a much higher interest rate than you ever expected. When you first signed up for the loan, you didn't fully grasp how challenging it would be to pay it off. Now, the weight of that debt is affecting your finances in ways you never anticipated.

High Interest Rates Puts You in a Vicious Cycle of Indebtedness

Higher interest rates mean that by the time you finish paying off your student loans, you'll have paid significantly more than you borrowed. This financial burden can be overwhelming, especially when you're just starting out and trying to build your career, buy a house, and start a family. Every month, a large chunk of your paycheck goes toward loan payments, leaving you with less money for other necessities and goals. It's a tough situation that many graduates face, making it harder to save for a house, invest in retirement, or even afford day-to-day expenses.

Is This Fair?

Education is crucial for personal and professional growth, and many believe it should be accessible to everyone. High interest rates on student loans can make it harder for people to afford the education they need, perpetuating cycles of debt and financial struggle.

Thinking About Solutions

Imagine you were going to college and needed a loan. How would you feel about paying a higher interest rate for your education compared to a loan for buying a house? Do you think it's fair, or should it be changed? What could be a better way to handle this? What if there were better ways to manage student loan interest rates? If the federal government is the lender, should the government provide the housing loan and student loan at the same interest rate?

CHAPTER 16

Why is the Federal Government in the Business of Student Loans?

Heading to college is an exciting time. You're about to embark on a journey filled with new learning and opportunities. But for many, this adventure starts with taking out a student loan backed by the federal government. It seems convenient—you can borrow enough to cover tuition and other expenses. But is it really as great as it sounds?

The federal government dominates the student loan market, providing billions in loans to students across the United States each year. While this system aims to make higher education accessible to everyone, it has some serious unintended consequences that worsen financial challenges for both students and educational institutions.

The Problem with Government-Backed Loans

- **Unlimited Lending:** Imagine a world where every time you wanted to buy something, someone was there to lend you the money, no questions asked. Sounds nice, right? But what if this meant prices kept climbing because sellers knew you could always borrow more? This is essentially what's happening in higher education. The government offers what amounts to a blank check to colleges by providing loans that cover any amount up to the full cost of attendance, which includes tuition, room, board, and other educational expenses.

- **Inflationary Pressure on Tuition:** Tuition rates have been rising much faster than inflation. Why? Because colleges know the government will always cover the bill through you. You graduate not just with a degree, but also with a mountain of debt that might take decades to pay off. Is that really supporting education? This easy access to funds removes the financial discipline that would normally keep tuition prices in check. Colleges are incentivized to increase fees because they know students can secure federal loans to pay for them.

- **Debt Burden on Graduates:** You graduate and are ready to start your life. But instead of saving for a house or starting a family, you're stuck paying off your student loans. How does that affect your life choices? How does it feel to be financially handcuffed right as you start your career? Graduates with substantial debt burdens often find it difficult to make significant life choices, like buying a home or starting a family.

The Economic and Social Implications

- **Economic Stagnation:** Burdened with debt, young adults are less likely to engage in economic activities that stimulate growth, such as entrepreneurship or home purchases.
- **Social Inequality:** The burden of debt disproportionately affects the middle class and poor. This exacerbates social inequalities and limits upward mobility.

How About Ending Federal Lending

- **Reduce Tuition Inflation:** Without the guarantee of federal loans, colleges would need to keep tuition rates within reason, aligned with what students can afford.
- **Promote Alternative Financing Methods:** Encouraging private lenders, scholarships, grants, and work-study programs might better align costs with the actual value and outcomes of educational programs.

Should Tuition be Linked to Economic Value the Colleges Provide?

Imagine a future where college tuition is directly linked to the economic value it provides, and students are free from the shackles of overwhelming debt. By stepping back from direct lending, the government can help correct the financial distortions in higher education. If you were to design a college financing system from scratch, what would you focus on? How would you ensure education is a stepping stone to success, not a path to financial burden?

CHAPTER 17

Why Does Car Towing Cost Almost the Value of Your Car?

You park briefly to drop off your child at his school. You think it will just take a minute. But when you return, your car is gone. Your car is towed away. You wonder on the street where to go and find the car and how big of a bill you are due to get your own car back. How did a simple school drop-off turn into a financial nightmare?

Why Are Towing Fees So High?

When your car is towed away, don't be surprised if the fine is more than the value of your car. You may wonder why small mistakes, in many cases forced by situation, are so expensive.

Why do towing fees cost so much? Well, it's because the system is designed to punish you badly. Often so bad that you end up losing your car. Arguably it includes towing labor, and distance and storage. These places are often located in inexpensive neighborhoods. People who work there rarely are well paid. But should these costs really add up to more than the car's value? In many places, with no caps on towing charges, fees can soar, leaving you with a bill that's tough to handle.

Are the Fees Reasonable?

Is it reasonable for towing companies to charge such high fees, especially when the tow wasn't for safety or emergency reasons? Sure, towing companies need to cover their costs and make a profit, but should those costs be as high as—or higher than—the value of the vehicles they tow? This balance between service costs and fairness often tips too far towards the former, leaving car owners with hefty bills.

Impact on People

Not everyone who gets their car towed is driving a fancy car or has a lot of money. Most people in America drive affordable cars. For many, a car is essential—for getting to work, school, or medical appointments. Exorbitant towing fees can threaten their ability to make ends meet, turning a minor parking mistake into a major financial crisis.

Thinking About Solutions

So, what's a reasonable approach? First, we need clearer, more prominently displayed parking regulations to prevent unnecessary tows. But there's more we can do:

- **Cap Towing Fees:** Cities and states should consider capping towing fees so they don't exceed a reasonable percentage of the car's value. No one should pay more for a tow than is justified.
- **Emergency-Only Towing:** Restrict towing to situations where a vehicle is truly causing an obstruction or is a safety hazard. This would prevent cars from being towed in non-emergency situations, where a fine would be more appropriate.

Reasonable Towing Practices

Unless your car is infringing upon the rights of someone else, imposing a monetary fine is likely a better approach instead of towing away the car. For example, if you are parked by a fire hydrant and there is a fire, does your car need to be removed, sure. If you are parked on a street where you are not supposed to park, is towing needed, perhaps not.

If reasonable limits on towing fees are imposed and if cars could be towed only when absolutely necessary, we can protect car owners from undue financial strain. It will discourage towing companies from actively soliciting towing opportunities. Maintaining order and safety of our streets are extremely important. However, we should also respect the financial realities of drivers. You would not find many people who are willing violators. Most people whose car was towed away were not intentionally creating a chaotic situation on the streets. Perhaps it was a lack of judgment or a necessity. If it were your car, your money, your life being disrupted by an unreasonable tow, what changes would you want to see? How can you balance the need for traffic control with fairness and compassion for all drivers?

CHAPTER 18

Why is Hospital Parking Cost So Expensive?

Imagine you must visit the hospital. Maybe you're dealing with a serious health diagnosis, or perhaps you're visiting a loved one who is ill. When you are visiting a hospital, you are obviously not super excited about it. It is not a leisure trip. You are often in anxiety and worried about health. Now, on top of this stress, you are being charged exorbitant fees just to park your car. Parking fees is an additional, unnecessary layer of stress and a financial burden especially when you are already stressed.

While much of the healthcare debate focuses on the direct costs of medical care—such as insurance premiums, copays, and medication costs—one frequently overlooked aspect is the cost of hospital parking. For many, especially those with limited financial means, parking fees can represent a significant and unavoidable financial burden. This complicates their access to necessary medical services.

Understanding the Impact of Parking Fees

Hospital parking fees can vary widely but are often exorbitantly high, particularly in urban areas where space is at a premium. These fees may seem like a minor inconvenience relative to other healthcare costs, but they can add up quickly, especially for patients requiring regular treatments such as chemotherapy or dialysis.

Disproportionate Impact on the Economically Vulnerable

- **Financial Burden:** For patients and families who are already struggling to cover medical bills, parking fees can be an additional stressor, sometimes costing hundreds of dollars a month.
- **Barrier to Regular Care:** High costs can deter patients from following through with needed regular care, potentially leading to worse health outcomes.
- **Punitive for Poor People:** The poorer you are, the more punitive these fees become. Wealthier patients may not notice the cost, but for those at the economic margins, even a few dollars can be a deterrent.

Case Studies and Real-Life Implications

- **Chronic Illness Patients:** Consider a patient undergoing regular cancer treatment who must visit the hospital multiple times a week for several hours each time. Parking fees alone can run into thousands of dollars annually.
- **Emergency Visits:** During emergencies, families might not have the luxury of searching for more affordable parking, resulting in high unexpected costs.

Arguments Against Hospital Parking Fees

- **Inequity:** Charging for parking at a place of care, especially when visits are not optional, is inherently inequitable. This practice can be seen as a form of regressive taxation, where those least able to pay feel the most significant impact.
- **Contrary to Medical Ethics:** The primary mission of healthcare providers is to do no harm. By imposing financial barriers to access, hospitals contradict their fundamental ethical commitments.
- **Reduced Patient Satisfaction:** High parking fees can lead to a negative overall healthcare experience, reducing patient satisfaction and potentially impacting hospital ratings and reputation.

Free Hospital Parking

1. **Reducing Stress:** Eliminating parking fees can significantly reduce the emotional and financial stress on patients and families. When you're worried about your health or a loved one's condition, the last thing

you should be stressing about is whether you can afford to park at the hospital.

2. **Making Healthcare Truly Accessible:** We often talk about making healthcare accessible, but accessibility isn't just about physical entry to a building; it's also about removing financial barriers. Free parking at hospitals should be a part of this broader initiative.

3. **A Gesture of Goodwill:** Hospitals aim to provide care and foster healing. Providing free parking could be seen as an extension of this care, a simple yet powerful gesture of goodwill towards those in need.

Hospital Parking Cost is Healthcare Cost

Imagine you need to make frequent hospital visits. How would free parking provided by the hospital impact your situation? As healthcare institutions continue to strive towards higher standards of patient care and equity, reevaluating the impact of parking fees is crucial. By addressing this often-overlooked aspect of healthcare access, hospitals can better align their operations with their ethical obligations and make healthcare truly accessible to all segments of society.

CHAPTER 19

Do You Know That Ambulance Bills May Not Be Covered By Your Health Insurance?

J enna is a young mother whose child suddenly becomes sick. She dials 911 and an ambulance arrives. The ambulance rushes her son to the hospital, potentially saving his life. Weeks later she receives a bill for over $4,000. Jenna calls the insurance company. The insurance company says that the ambulance charges are covered only for $500. Jenna calls the ambulance provider. They tell her there is nothing they can do. Jenna must pay. She doesn't have the money to pay. The bill goes to the collection agency.

What if you were in Jenna's shoes? You exercised your best judgment in calling an ambulance. Why such a hefty bill then that no one wants to pay? This situation raises several critical questions: How can we ensure that people aren't penalized for needing urgent care? How would Jenna know which ambulance provider is covered by her insurance when she dialed 911?

The Unexpected Insurance Gap

Most people assume that their health insurance will cover emergency transport costs. However, you might be shocked to discover that many health insurance policies have significant gaps when it comes to ambulance services. Sometimes, they only cover a fraction of the total cost, or worse, none at all.

Thousands of Dollars for a Ride

Why are ambulance services treated differently than other medical expenses? It turns out that ambulance services often operate under different billing frameworks, which are not always fully integrated with health insurance plans. This can lead to a major headache when the bill arrives, showing charges that can run into thousands of dollars.

There are many stories of people who received ambulance bills for thousands of dollars after their insurance refused to pay. These bills can be a huge burden, especially if the person thought their insurance would cover the cost.

What Can Be Done?

Imagine you or someone in your family needed an ambulance, but later you got a bill that was more than you could afford. What would you think about the cost of emergency services? How do you think we can make this system fairer for everyone? This situation raises important questions about how emergency medical services should be funded and managed. Should there be more regulation on ambulance billing? Should insurance always cover these costs? What's the best way to make sure people can get emergency help without facing huge bills later? Perhaps it's time for clearer regulations on ambulance billing, or for insurance policies to mandatorily cover emergency transport costs.

CHAPTER 20

Why is Medical Debt Not Excluded from Collection and Credit Reporting

You wake up in the middle of the night with severe chest pain. Frightened, you rush to the emergency room, where doctors perform several tests and stabilize your condition. Relief washes over you as you realize you've survived what could have been a heart attack. But then, weeks later, a new kind of shock arrives in the mail: a massive medical bill that your insurance only partially covers. You're suddenly thrust into a financial emergency caused by a health emergency.

Medical debt is unlike any other form of debt. It often comes out of nowhere. It is incredibly expensive and isn't fully understood by patients when they receive care. The complexity and opacity of healthcare billing can leave patients feeling overwhelmed by high medical bills they never saw coming.

Understanding Medical Debt

You receive a bill that's far beyond what you can afford. You know there's no way you'll be able to pay it off. Then the collection agency starts calling, threatening not just your finances but your credit score. This could make it harder for you to buy a house, get a car, or even secure a job. It's a vicious cycle where your physical health crisis leads to a financial crisis, which then loops back to affect your overall well-being.

Why Medical Debt Shouldn't Damage Your Credit

Medical debt isn't like buying a luxury item you can't afford; it's often an unavoidable consequence of seeking necessary, sometimes life-saving, medical care. Here's what makes medical debt so uniquely burdensome:

- **Unpredictability and Necessity**: You don't plan to get sick or injured. Medical debt can arise from circumstances entirely beyond your control, unlike debts from planned expenditures. For example, Alex is riding his bike as usual. A car hits him while making a turn. Alex is taken to the emergency at a nearby hospital. The hospital is an out-of-network provider in Alex's health insurance plan. Alex gets a bill of $17,000.

Alex is not able to pay off the debt. His credit is damaged.

- **Opaque Billing Practices**: Often, you don't know the cost of services until after you've received them, and you're hardly in a position to negotiate or shop around when undergoing treatment. Imagine in Alex's case, what choice he had when he got into a bike accident? He couldn't call ten hospitals and get a bargain.

- **Insurance Dependence**: Even with insurance, the maze of copays, deductibles, and exclusions can leave you with substantial bills. The final amount you owe can swing wildly based on how insurance companies assess your claims, a process fraught with delays and denials that are also out of your control. Revisiting Alex's case, he would not even know how much the medical treatment would cost and whether insurance will cover it fully or not.

- **Involuntary Debt**: Unlike other debts incurred from voluntary purchases, medical debt can accumulate without your consent or control, often in life-or-death situations. For example, Maria is a first-time mother-to-be. When she is admitted at the hospital, she expects a normal pregnancy However, it turns out the pregnancy would be far more complicated. Maria walked out front from the hospital with her baby. After a few days she gets a surprise $30,000 hospital bill. Despite having insurance, she found that many of the charges were not covered. Her credit score plummeted as she struggled to manage this debt, affecting her family's ability to secure a future home loan.

Impacts of Medical Debt

- **Credit Damage**: Medical debt can severely impact your credit score, affecting your ability to buy a home, secure loans, or even gain employment.
- **Financial Instability**: The burden of unexpected medical bills can push individuals and families into financial hardship or bankruptcy.
- **Health Consequences**: The stress associated with medical debt can worsen health issues, ironically making recovery harder.

Medical Health Should Not Ruin Your Family's Financial Health

Medical debt should not be treated like other forms of consumer debt. It's a byproduct of circumstances often beyond anyone's control. By removing medical debt from debt collection and credit reporting practices, we can protect patients from the undue stress and financial instability that currently accompanies many medical treatments.

Have you or someone close to you been overwhelmed by medical debt? How did it affect your life choices and financial stability?

CHAPTER 21

Does Charging for Plastic Bags Really Decrease Environmental Waste?

You're checking out at a grocery store. The cashier asks if you need a bag. You didn't bring your reusable ones today, so you say yes. That's when they tell you there's a charge for the plastic bag. It's just a few cents, but it's meant to discourage you from using single-use plastics, which are arguably bad for the environment. But have you ever wondered if charging for these bags genuinely decreases waste, or if it just shifts the problem elsewhere?

The Intended Green Benefit

The idea behind charging for plastic bags is straightforward: by making them a paid item, people will think twice before using them. This will help reduce waste and encourage shoppers to bring reusable bags. It sounds great in theory, right? Less plastic equals less pollution. But let's dig a little deeper.

Unintended Consequences

When stores start charging for plastic bags, something unexpected happens. Instead of switching to reusable bags, many people just buy different types of single-use bags. Have you noticed thicker, more durable bags popping up at your store? They're often marketed as "reusable," but they require even more resources to produce and can be worse for the environment if not reused enough.

The Rebound Effect

Think about what you do with those lightweight grocery bags. Many people use them as trash bin liners or to pick up after pets. When you don't have these bags anymore because you're avoiding the charge, you end up buying heavier, plastic trash bags. So, in a twist of irony, we might end up using more plastic.

Economic and Social Impact

Think about the broader implications. Every additional charge on a plastic bag or bottle can deter a low-income shopper from making necessary purchases or add to their financial strain. What is intended as a nudge towards environmental consciousness can feel more like a financial penalty to those already under economic stress.

The extra charge on bags can also be a burden for those on tight budgets. Every penny counts, and what's meant as a nudge towards better habits can feel like a penalty to those who are already struggling. Not everyone can easily absorb these additional costs. For individuals on fixed incomes, such as those receiving SNAP benefits, the elderly, or anyone living paycheck to paycheck, these small charges can accumulate quickly, becoming a significant financial burden.

Beyond Bags to Bottles and Other Plastics

It's not just plastic bags. Charges on plastic bottles and other containers add up too. For many, especially those who can't easily access bulk buying or higher-priced eco-friendly alternatives, these costs are unavoidable. This raises a critical question: Is it fair to disproportionately penalize those who are least able to pay?

Promoting Environment Should Not Be Financially Punitive

As we strive to protect our planet, we must also consider the fairness of our methods. The next time you pay for a plastic bag or bottle, think about the wider impact of that policy. Is it truly a step towards a greener planet, or does it impose an unfair burden on those who can least afford it? Next time you're asked if you need a bag and whether you're willing to pay for it, think about what that charge represents. Is it a step toward a greener planet, or is it another punitive finance for people who are poor?

THREE

TAXES

CHAPTER 22

Why Can't Everyone Pay Their Share of Taxes?

Imagine a world where everyone contributes the same percentage of their income in taxes—whether they earn a lot or a little. It sounds pretty fair, right? In this system, whether you're Sam making $1 million or Jack earning $100,000, you both pay the same rate, say 10%. This means your contribution is valued equally in the eyes of society, regardless of your income.

The Principle of Equality

Under a flat tax system, everyone pays the same slice of their income. This simplifies tax obligations and emphasizes that every citizen has an equal stake in funding public services. Here's why this could be a more just approach:

- **Simplicity and Transparency:** Everyone understands what they owe. There's no confusion about varying tax brackets or deductions, making the tax system easier to navigate and harder to manipulate.
- **Encouraging Fairness and Participation:** When everyone pays the same rate, it fosters a sense of fairness and collective responsibility. This could increase civic engagement as people feel more directly connected to where their taxes are going and how they are used.
- **Removing Disincentives to Earn More:** In a progressive tax system, higher earners might feel penalized for their success with higher tax rates. A flat tax removes these disincentives, potentially encouraging more economic activity and entrepreneurship.

Economic Impact

With a flat tax, the economy could benefit from increased transparency and reduced bureaucracy. For Sam and Jack, paying 10% means they know exactly how much they owe without complex calculations. This clarity can lead to better financial planning and investment, fueling economic growth.

Equitable Contributions

Look at the fairness. Sam's 10% might be a larger amount in dollars compared to Jack's, but proportionally, their sacrifice is the same. Each person is contributing equally to the society according to their means, without unduly burdening or benefiting one group over another.

Potential Challenges and Solutions

Some people argue that a flat tax hurts people who earn less. As a result, the government offers several exemptions. However, as the other chapters argue in this book, the government can fully fund critical things such as childcare, transportation, education, and food which would eliminate the need of claiming for exemptions which many tax filers do not claim anyways since they are not able to afford an expensive tax preparer.

Building Fair Tax System

Think about how you would feel knowing that everyone, regardless of their wealth, pays the same percentage of their income. Does this change your perception of fairness and equality in society? How might this influence your decisions if you were to start a business or manage your own finances?

CHAPTER 23

Will Eliminating Non-Profit's 501(c)(3) Tax Deduction Loophole Solve Nearly All Problems in this World?

When you heard rich people like Bill Gates donating his wealth away, you celebrated his generosity. People like Warren Buffet gave away nearly all his company. Guess what, these donations simply mean the money or stocks these people owned were transferred to a non-profit company they or their close people controlled. Warren Buffett donated to the Bill and Melinda Gates Foundation. Bill Gates also donated to his own non-profit. Well, you shouldn't be surprised to know that Bill and Melinda Gates Foundation's assets are mostly the stocks of Warren

Buffet's company Berkshire Hathaway and Bill Gates' company Microsoft. Does this large ownership influence the stock price of their own companies? Of course! This setup means that while Buffett's and Gates' charitable giving helps the foundation's mission, it simultaneously boosts their financial interests.

The Birth of 501(c)(3)

The legal framework for tax-exempt status under Section 501(c)(3) of the Internal Revenue Code traces its roots back to the early 20th century. Its inception was motivated by a desire to support and encourage philanthropic activities by offering tax exemptions to organizations that engage exclusively in charitable, religious, scientific, or educational endeavors. The idea was simple: to foster a culture of giving and provide societal benefits by relieving charitable organizations from the burden of tax obligations.

Noble Intentions

The establishment of 501(c)(3) status was grounded in the belief that non-profit organizations play a crucial role in addressing societal issues, filling gaps that neither the government nor the private sector could adequately cover. By providing tax exemptions, the law aimed to channel more resources towards public service and philanthropy, thereby enriching the social, cultural, and educational fabric of American society.

The Slippery Slope to Abuse

However, what started as a policy to promote genuine philanthropy has, over the years, been manipulated and exploited by some wealthy individuals and entities. The crux of the abuse lies in the ability to transfer assets into a 501(c)(3) organization, effectively shielding these assets from taxation, while the donors continue to exert control over how these assets are utilized.

The Mechanics of Misuse

Consider the mechanics of these charitable contributions. A wealthy individual transfers substantial sums from their personal or corporate accounts into a tax-exempt non-profit organization they control. On paper, it's a generous donation. In reality, it's a strategic shift of resources that remain under the donor's influence. This setup allows them to use these funds to further personal, business, or political objectives, leveraging the charity's assets to support interconnected businesses and initiatives.

Example of Strategic 'Donations'

Donations have become very strategic now. Imagine a billionaire who donates $100 million to a university through his non-profit organization. The headline screams generosity, but the details tell a different story. The university, in turn, spends double that amount purchasing products and services from the billionaire's for-profit company. The company's stock value skyrockets, and the billionaire's wealth increases, all while enjoying a tax break meant for genuine charitable activities.

There are numerous examples of this. Bill Gates donated to universities such as Harvard or Cambridge and those institutions buy Microsoft products. Warren Buffet invested in his own company Berkshire Hathaway but by transferring his ownership to a non-profit entity. The non-profit bought millions of dollars' worth of stock in companies like Coca-Cola and McDonald's. These purchases not only boost the stock prices of these companies, some owned by Berkshire Hathaway. Mark Zuckerberg pledged his Facebook shares to the Chan Zuckerberg Initiative (CZI), a company that he controls. This allows for more control over investments and political lobbying, blending philanthropy with significant personal and financial influence. For instance, CZI can invest in for-profit startups, political causes, and social movements that align with Zuckerberg's interests and values, effectively allowing him to shape public discourse and policy while enjoying substantial tax benefits. George Soros donated his money to his own non-profit Open Society Foundations to fund various initiatives that align with his political views, leveraging philanthropy for significant influence on public policy and global affairs.

Non-Profits Create Dark Money Cycle

Beyond individual gain, these tax-exempt organizations can become conduits for what's known as dark money. Funds can circulate among various entities, supporting nepotism and extending influence without transparency or accountability.

This opaque movement of money can distort public policy and exacerbate inequality, all sheltered under the umbrella of nonprofit activity. Imagine tracing money among various entities and who is funding what. In most cases, the names of the donors are not public and even if they are, they are shielded with non-profit entities names, not individual names which makes it impossible for anyone to find who is behind a cause, whether good or bad, that's funded by tax-sheltered money.

Why Elimination Is Necessary

It is increasingly visible that 501c(3) "donations" are less about charity and more about maintaining control and influence, all while reaping substantial tax benefits. It's time to question whether the 501(c)(3) tax exemption, as it currently stands, serves the public good or merely facilitates private gains under the guise of philanthropy. By eliminating these exemptions, we could:

- Reduce the incentive for using charities as personal tax shelters.
- Increase transparency in philanthropic funding.
- Ensure that charitable activities are genuinely independent and focused on public benefit rather than private advantage.

Redefining Philanthropy

True philanthropy does not need the lure of tax relief. Many of history's most revered philanthropists gave without such incentives, driven by a genuine desire to improve the world. If the primary motive for giving is tax avoidance or personal gain, it's not charity; it's business. Instead of merely adjusting the regulations around 501(c)(3), perhaps it's time to rethink the entire framework to better align with the original spirit of charitable giving. If the intentions are noble, people will donate whether there is any tax exemption or not.

Have you ever wondered how much of charitable giving is driven by genuine intent versus financial incentives? How might our understanding of philanthropy change if tax benefits were removed from the equation?

CHAPTER 24

Why Do You Have to Pay Sales Tax on Used Products?

You're at your local used car dealership. You are thrilled to find a decent car that fits your tight budget. You settle on a five-year-old sedan priced at $10,000. You think it's a bargain compared to a new model. Then you see a whopping amount in sales tax that you must pay. Your great deal isn't quite as great after the government adds its share. You wonder why a car that was taxed when it was sold previously is being taxed again just for changing hands.

In many places, buying used products—whether cars, furniture, or electronics—means paying sales tax, just like when you buy something new. This practice means that every time an item changes hands in the marketplace, the state collects sales tax on its sale.

Understanding the Mechanics of Used Product Taxation

Taxing used products imposes multiple tax burdens on a single item as it depreciates in value. Let's break it down with a simple example:

- **Initial Purchase**: John buys a new Ford F150 for $20,000 and pays a 10% sales tax, adding $2,000 to the cost of the vehicle.
- **First Resale**: Two years later, John sells the truck to Mary for $15,000. Mary pays a 10% sales tax on this amount, which amounts to $1,500.
- **Second Resale**: Mary sells the truck a year later to Joe for $10,000. Joe again pays a 10% sales tax, adding another $1,000 to the cost.

Over the life of this single vehicle, the state collects a total of $4,500 in sales taxes from three different owners, despite the vehicle's depreciating value. This example shows how sales taxes on used products can disproportionately affect consumers, particularly those in lower income brackets who are more likely to buy used items.

Economic and Social Implications

The taxation of used goods has several negative consequences:

- **Double Taxation**: The same item is taxed multiple times, which is essentially a form of double taxation—a concept generally opposed on principles of tax fairness and efficiency.
- **Regressive Impact**: Because lower-income individuals are more likely to buy used goods, the impact of these taxes is regressive, disproportionately affecting those least able to afford them.

A Fairer Approach?

What if used items weren't taxed? Could this encourage more people to buy used, helping both their wallets and the environment?

- **Boosting the Second-hand Market**: Making used goods more affordable could revitalize local markets and online platforms, promoting a culture of reuse.
- **Supporting Lower Income Families**: If you're trying to make ends meet, every penny counts. Reducing taxes on used items could be a direct way to support families in stretching their budgets further.

Taxation on Used Products is Unnecessary

Imagine a world where the tax code supports, rather than penalizes, smart consumer choices like buying used. What could that look like, and how would it change your shopping habits? Would it encourage you to choose used items more often, knowing that you're not only saving money but also reducing waste?

FOUR

ELECTIONS

CHAPTER 25

Why Are The Election District Maps Drawn So Illogically?

Have you ever looked at a map of congressional districts? You expect some simple geometric shapes. Instead, what you see looks like a jigsaw puzzle gone wrong: strange nonsensical shapes sprawling in all directions, cutting through cities and splitting neighborhoods. This is poor mapping by design. It's called "gerrymandering,". It is a manipulative practice aimed at securing political advantages for a particular party or candidate. The district lines are drawn in a way to make sure whoever is drawing it keeps winning. This practice is used by both major political parties. It undermines the foundational principles of democratic representation. You wonder: shouldn't the shapes of these districts make sense?

The Problem with Gerrymandering

There are many districts in this country that are considered "safe" districts. It means the favored party will win no matter what. This practice of gerrymandering involves drawing electoral district boundaries to favor one party, effectively predetermining electoral outcomes and stifling competition. It affects how your votes count and who represents you. This manipulation leads to several critical issues:

- **Power Plays:** By drawing boundaries to include or exclude specific groups, politicians can almost guarantee their party's victory in that district, sidelining a fair competition.
- **Echo Chambers:** Safe districts create echo chambers where only the most extreme voices get heard, pushing politicians further from the center.
- **Distrust and Disillusionment:** When you see a district that snakes along highways and splits apart communities, it's hard not to feel like the system is rigged. This erodes trust in democratic processes and discourages people from voting.

The Case for Rational Districts

You might wonder why these maps aren't just straightforward. Here's why rational shapes make sense:

- **Fair Play:** Logical, straightforward districts make sure everyone's vote has equal power, which is how democracy is supposed to work.

- **Better Leadership:** When districts are drawn fairly, politicians have to appeal to a broader range of voters and work harder to represent their interests, which can lead to more balanced and effective governance.
- **Restoring Trust:** Clear, rational district maps can help restore faith in the electoral system. When voters see districts that make sense, they can feel more confident that their voices are heard and matter.

Geometrically Defined Districts

Currently, our electoral districts often serve the best interests of political maneuvering. Imagine if instead, we approached districting with a commitment to geometric fairness, where each district is shaped based on clear, mathematical principles rather than political strategy.

Why not divide states into districts with shapes as regular and geometrically even as possible? For instance, take Oklahoma— a state with a specific number of electoral votes. We could divide it into districts that are geometrically equal, each resembling slices of a pie or regular polygons, depending on the total area and population requirements. This method would not only simplify the boundaries but also make them inherently fairer, ensuring that each district is equal in size and shape, minimizing the chances of any one group wielding undue influence over the others.

Making Sense of the Map

The arbitrary and manipulated shapes of today's congressional districts serve the interests of political parties, not the public. With districts designed to respect geometric equality, every voter's influence is balanced, and the focus shifts back to genuine representation and policy-making. How would this approach change your engagement with the electoral process? Would knowing that your district is designed to ensure fairness inspire more confidence and participation in our democracy?

CHAPTER 26

Why Not Give a Day Off to Vote on Election Day?

Imagine it's Election Day. You're an hourly worker at a busy sandwich shop. Your shift starts at 8 AM and ends at 6 PM, just as the polls close. You've been up since 5 AM, juggling the morning rush, and there's no way to get to your polling place during your short break. By the time you finish your shift, exhausted and frustrated, you realize you've missed your chance to vote. This scenario is a reality for many Americans, highlighting a crucial problem in our democratic process.

The Case for Paid Time Off on Election Day

Think back to that long day at the restaurant. You were eager to vote, but the pressures of your job made it impossible. If

Election Day were a paid holiday, you wouldn't have to choose between earning a day's wage and fulfilling your civic duty.

Challenges with Alternative Voting Methods

Many argue that mail-in voting offers the convenience for the people who wouldn't be available to vote on Election Day. However, this is a contagious proposition. It would be impossible to convince all Americas that voting by mail is safe no matter what the government does. Mail-in-ballot has created a gravest mistrust in the voting process and further erosion of trust in election is the single biggest threat to rule of people, the very foundation of America. Plus, there's something uniquely communal about showing up in person to vote, a shared national moment that mail-in voting doesn't quite capture.

Benefits of Results by Evening

Giving everyone the day off to vote could also lead to faster vote tallying. Imagine election nights where the majority of votes are cast and counted on the same day, restoring the excitement and immediacy to the process that can be lost in prolonged counts.

Ensuring Universal Access to Voting

It's all about including all Americans in the voting process. By providing paid time off to vote, employers would play a direct role in supporting democracy. This change could lead to more participation across all demographics, especially among those who might skip voting due to economic pressures.

Election Day Holiday Will Increase Voter Participation

Having paid time off to vote would significantly increase voter participation, ensuring that more voices are heard in our democracy. Making Election Day a paid holiday isn't just about convenience; it's about strengthening our democracy by ensuring every citizen has the opportunity to participate fully. This simple change could transform voter turnout and enthusiasm, making our democratic process more inclusive and fairer for everyone.

Now, imagine yourself in a supportive environment where you can vote without the pressure of work. How would it change your Election Day experience? Would this make you more enthusiastic about voting? Reflect on your past voting experiences. Was it stressful finding time to vote around your work schedule? Would having a day off have made the process easier and more enjoyable for you?

CHAPTER 27

Is an Identification Card Really Difficult to Get?

Imagine you're trying to enter a government building for a scheduled appointment for Social Security. You are stopped at the entrance to show your ID. Or you are asked to show your ID at the postal office when you go to pick up your own package. You are used to showing your ID regardless of whether you find it inconvenient or frustrating. Now when you go to vote, you are not asked for an ID. You wonder why you are asked for an ID even for small things but not for the most important event in a democracy. If you need an ID for basic tasks like picking up a package or entering a building, is it really unreasonable to require one for voting?

The Reality of ID Access

In modern times, it's nearly impossible to find people who do not have an identification card. Most people have drivers licenses and if they are not drivers, they at least have the State ID. Yet, requiring IDs for voting has sparked significant debate.

ID Establishes Trust

In the fabric of democratic society, nothing is more vital than the citizen's faith in the election process. People who vote, especially the ones whose candidates lose, must believe the election was fair. If people don't believe the election is fair, then democracy doesn't function. Voter ID laws, which require individuals to present identification before voting, are often seen as a contentious issue. However, when considering the routine nature of ID checks in everyday life, requiring identification to vote not only minimizes potential fraud but also strengthens public confidence in elections.

Historical Context and Modern Relevance

In the past, particularly during the segregation era, discriminatory practices severely restricted the voting rights of certain groups, most notably African-Americans. Today, ensuring that everyone who is eligible to vote can do so should be coupled with measures that secure the vote itself:

- **Learning from the Past:** Stories from those who lived through segregation emphasize the transformative power of gaining the right to vote. With this right now secured, the focus must shift to protecting the integrity of each vote through sensible measures like ID requirements.

- **Enhanced Accessibility:** Modern voter ID laws should be designed to enhance, not hinder, voting accessibility. Provisions should be made to issue IDs free of charge and facilitate easy access to ID registration.

The Necessity of Voter ID

- **Preventing Fraud:** Voter ID laws serve as a practical measure to prevent fraudulent activities in elections, ensuring that each vote cast is legitimate.
- **Boosting Confidence:** By securing the voting process against fraud, voter IDs help maintain electoral integrity, which in turn boosts confidence among voters and candidates about the fairness and outcomes of elections.
- **Standard Practice:** Everyday activities, such as boarding an airplane, entering secure buildings, or making transactions at the bank, all require valid identification. Extending this standard practice to voting ensures uniformity in how identification is used to secure and facilitate important civic processes.

Addressing Concerns and Safeguards

People who don't want voters to show IDs argue that asking for an ID can disenfranchise certain voters, particularly minorities. If that is true, those concerns can be addressed effectively:

- **Accountability in Enforcement:** Election officials who do not allow certain qualified voters not to vote should face strict penalties. Safeguards must be in place to prevent and address any form of disenfranchisement or discrimination.

- **Proactive Government Role:** The government should play a proactive role in ensuring that all eligible voters can obtain the necessary IDs. This involves outreach programs, mobile registration units, and other community-based initiatives that help bridge any gaps in access to identification.

Government Initiatives for Accessible ID Provision

To further mitigate any barriers to obtaining a voter ID, governments at all levels should undertake significant efforts to provide State IDs or Driver's Licenses at no cost to the individuals:

- **Free State IDs:** Offering free State IDs to all eligible voters would remove a significant financial barrier to voter participation. This initiative should be well-publicized and easily accessible.

- **Extensive Outreach:** Implementing mobile ID units that travel to underserved areas can help ensure that all citizens, especially those in remote or marginalized communities, can obtain their IDs without undue hardship.

- **Educational Campaigns:** Widespread public education on the importance of voter IDs and how to obtain them should be a priority.
- **Community Partnerships:** Collaborations between election commissions and community organizations can help facilitate the distribution of IDs and provide voters with the information they need.

Launch Free USA Voter ID to Prevent Abuse

In order to increase voter participation and prevent abuse, the government can launch a "USA Voter ID" program, free of cost. This ID would be used solely for voting purposes. Many countries have already implemented similar programs with success. Providing a free, dedicated voter ID increases trust in the electoral system and ensures that no one is left without the means to participate in elections.

Voter ID Requirements Will Strengthen Democracy

Think about the last time you needed an ID. Was it a hassle, or just part of routine procedure? Or was it an inconvenience that you didn't like? How would ensuring everyone shows an ID at the polls change your perception of election legitimacy? Would knowing that every voter is verified in the same way you were change your confidence in the electoral process?

CHAPTER 28

Should Non-Citizens Influence Congressional Redistricting?

Imagine you live in a neighborhood where the decisions about your schools, roads, and policies are influenced by the number of people around you. Now, consider that many of these people aren't eligible to vote. This is the reality in the United States. Congressional districts are drawn and electoral votes allocated based on total population, including non-citizens. This means non-citizens indirectly influence federal elections. This raises the question: Should non-citizens influence these critical aspects of democracy?

Understanding Apportionment and Its Impacts

Apportionment shapes our democracy. It determines how many representatives each state gets in Congress and how many electoral votes they have in presidential elections. Right now, this process counts everyone, where you are an eligible citizen to vote or not. Here's why this matters:

- **Congressional Redistricting:** More representatives might go to areas with larger populations, regardless of how many people there can actually vote. For example, in your city of one million population, you may have over a hundred thousand non-citizens. That's well over ten percent of the people who are changing the outcome of an election.
- **Electoral College Influence:** Some states might end up with more influence in presidential elections, again not directly reflecting the voter base. For example, if the state of California has ten percent non-voting eligible citizens but they are counted in the census, then California gets extra representatives in government and also extra seats for the presidential election. Not to mention, more dollar allocation to the state by the federal government.

Ensuring Non-Voters Don't Affect Elections

States with large non-citizen populations often receive more congressional and electoral college representation. This encourages politicians to flood their states with illegal immigrants. However, this action does not accurately reflect the voting population's size or political intentions. This directly affects the integrity of the election. The presence of non-citizens in the census count used for political redistricting skews political power and electoral outcomes in ways that do not correspond to the nation's electorate.

One way to prevent non-citizens from affecting elections is to directly review how many people are enrolled in Voter ID. As mentioned in the previous chapter, Voter ID will ensure only citizens are counted for apportionment. Another way is for the courts to clarify the rules specifying the exclusion of non-citizens from apportionment calculations. Furthermore, states can adopt apportionment bases for their legislative districts that reflect their citizen populations, potentially setting a precedent for federal action.

Ensuring Voter Only Representation

When non-citizens significantly impact the drawing of political boundaries and the allocation of electoral representation, it challenges the principles of fair representation. By reconsidering how we count populations for these purposes, we can ensure that every voter's voice is equally valued and that policies reflect the desires of actual constituents. Knowing that another state has more representatives because they have a significant percentage of non-voters, how does that affect your vote? What other measures could be taken to ensure fair representation in U.S. elections? Could this change lead to better alignment between community needs and governmental actions?

CHAPTER 29

Why are Elected Officials Not Granted Political Immunity to Safeguard Democracy?

Imagine the downfall of Ancient Rome. Political opponents were often prosecuted and executed, leading to an environment where power was maintained through fear rather than fair governance. This kind of political suppression isn't just ancient history. Consider Brazil's recent turmoil, where former leaders are prosecuted by new administrations, often in a pattern that seems more about politics than justice. Or take Pakistan, where no elected Prime Minister has been spared by the opposition party when it assumes power, often resulting in imprisonment or execution. Even in established democracies, the prosecution of political opponents is a recurring threat, as evident in the U.S. with Joe Biden's prosecution of his political opponent Donald Trump. This global issue raises a critical question: Could granting political immunity to elected officials be a solution to protect democracy?

Mechanisms of Political Suppression

Judicial Manipulation: In several countries, ruling parties exploit the judiciary to incapacitate opposition. For instance, in recent cases, America's Democratic Party President Joe Biden and his party's prosecutors brought numerous charges against the 45th President of the United States, Donald Trump, who is also Biden's main political opponent. This erodes trust in the American judicial system and highlights how justice can be weaponized for political gain.

Abuse of Law Enforcement: Law enforcement agencies often act as instruments of political power. Under Robert Mugabe's regime in Zimbabwe, police and security forces frequently targeted opposition members with arrests and intimidation, stifling dissent and maintaining Mugabe's grip on power.

Legislative Tools: Laws ostensibly designed to maintain order, such as those against "unrest" or "foreign interference," can be manipulated to suppress legitimate political activities. In Hong Kong, the National Security Law has been used to quash pro-democracy movements, demonstrating how legislative tools can be twisted to serve authoritarian ends.

Historical and Contemporary Examples

From the British Empire using judiciary as a show trial to arrest and execute freedom-seeking Indians to flawed democracies such as Brazil and the United States where laws are selectively enforced by the ruling party to disadvantage the opposition, the misuse of legal systems is a clear and present danger to democratic integrity.

Absolute Immunity

Scope of Immunity: Implementing absolute immunity would shield opposition politicians from politically motivated prosecutions, allowing them to participate in political activities without fear of retribution. This would not extend to violent crimes, ensuring that severe offenses still face accountability.

Rationale: This immunity could help maintain a balance of power by preventing the ruling party from using legal means to eliminate political threats. By focusing political battles in the electoral arena rather than courtrooms, we can foster a healthier democratic process.

Challenges

The primary concern with granting such immunity is the potential for non-violent corruption to go unchecked. Without the threat of legal consequences, some politicians might exploit their positions for personal gain. Striking a balance between protection from political persecution and accountability for corruption is essential.

Potential Benefits and Drawbacks

Benefits: Immunity would prevent the judiciary from being used as a tool for political control, promoting a more competitive and transparent political environment. It would also reassure the public that legal actions against politicians are not merely politically motivated.

Drawbacks: The major downside is that immunity could protect unethical behavior that doesn't involve violence, presenting a significant challenge. Ensuring that immunity does not become a shield for criminality is a complex but necessary task.

Exploring Democratic Safeguards

Imagine if your preferred political leader was suddenly charged with a non-violent crime by the ruling leader. Would you believe it was a fair application of the law or suspect political manipulation? To maintain trust in the system, it's crucial to ensure that the judiciary remains impartial and that legal processes are not abused for political gains.

The debate over political immunity is complex. While it can protect against judicial abuse, it also risks sheltering corrupt practices. The challenge lies in creating a system that defends democratic principles without offering a free pass for criminal behavior. As we explore these solutions, we must aim to protect the integrity of our political system, ensuring that every action upholds fairness and justice. What measures can we implement to balance these concerns effectively, and how can we safeguard democracy while promoting accountability? These questions are vital to preserving the true spirit of our democratic values.

CHAPTER 30

Why are Politicians Allowed to Remove Someone Who is Elected by the People?

You cast your vote for Daniel as your congressman, drawn in by his vision for your community. Politicians and the government accuse him of wrongdoing midway through his term. Despite accusations of wrongdoing, you still stand by him because you believe in his issues and you believe he is not treated well because he has the will to challenge the system as an outsider. Yet, Congress steps in and decides to remove her. Just like that, your choice—your voice—is dismissed by people who don't even represent your district. How would that make you feel? It's almost as if your vote, and what you thought it stood for, doesn't count at all.

When you cast your vote for someone, you're participating in a sacred transaction of democracy. You're choosing a representative to voice your concerns and stand for your interests. However, current protocols allow congressional bodies to dismiss these elected officials, raising critical questions about the respect for and validity of your electoral choice.

Congress holds the power to expel members with a two-thirds vote in cases like corruption or other severe breaches of trust. This rule is meant to protect the integrity of the institution but think about its implications. Could this power be misused? Could it undermine the very foundation of voter trust and choice?

Arguments Against Congressional Removal

- **Erosion of Voter Sovereignty:** If Congress can simply overturn the election of an official, what does that say about the value of your vote? It suggests that your choice is only temporary unless confirmed continuously by those in power.
- **Potential for Partisan Abuse:** Imagine Congress using this power to systematically remove opposition members. This possibility can turn a tool meant for accountability into a weapon of political warfare.
- **Contradiction to Democratic Principles:** At its core, democracy is about the power deriving from the consent of the governed—that's you, the voters—not their elected peers.

The Case for Voter-Only Removal

- **Direct Accountability:** Only allowing voters to remove their officials directly via recall elections or other mechanisms ensures that these leaders answer to you, not just to other politicians.
- **Reduces Partisan Manipulations:** It minimizes the risk that internal political strategies or vendettas dictate who gets to serve, preserving the integrity of electoral outcomes.
- **Upholds Democratic Ideals:** Emphasizing voter-only removal reiterates that in a democracy, real power should lie with the people, not nested within layers of political maneuvering.

Reaffirming Voter Primacy in Democracy

Ultimately, the power to hire and fire elected officials should rest where it began: with you, the voter. Strengthening this principle supports the very bedrock of democratic governance and ensures that elected representatives truly reflect the will of the people they serve. How do you think democracies can balance effective governance and ethical conduct with the need to respect the voters' choice? What systems would you design to ensure that politicians remain accountable to the electorate above all?

CHAPTER 31

Why is Out of State Donation Allowed to Influence Your State's Elections?

Imagine you're a lifelong resident of Missouri, deeply connected to its schools, economy, and community. Motivated by a desire to effect positive change, you decide to run for Congress to represent your state's unique needs and values. Your campaign starts with optimism and a community-driven spirit, but soon, a disconcerting reality emerges.

Your main opponent has spent most of his life in California but is contesting the same Missouri congressional seat. Strikingly, the bulk of his campaign funding comes from donors in California, not Missouri. These donors are drawn to him not for his grasp of Missouri's issues but because he supports policies that align with their ideologies. These policies might not resonate with or even benefit the people of Missouri. He manages to secure ten times the amount of money you can raise, overpowering your campaign with sheer financial might. This scenario raises pressing questions: Why is this allowed? Why are people who don't live in your state allowed to donate to political candidates in your state?

The Problem with Out-of-State Donations

Out-of-state political donations have become a pivotal aspect of campaign financing in many electoral contests across the United States. While these contributions can help candidates fund robust campaigns, they also introduce a potential for significant external influence, overshadowing local voters' preferences and needs.

- **Impact on Local Representation:** Candidates with substantial out-of-state funding might prioritize the interests of their distant donors over the constituents they aim to represent. This can lead to policies that do not address local issues effectively or authentically.
- **Potential for Misaligned Values:** When out-of-state interests dictate the political and financial landscape of a campaign, there is a risk that the elected officials will be more attuned to the needs and values of their financiers rather than those of their electorate.

Why Reform Is Necessary

The current situation necessitates a reevaluation of how electoral campaigns are funded and the sources of this funding. Here's what needs to be considered:

- **Promoting Local Interests:** Campaign finance reform could restrict out-of-state donations, ensuring that local candidates remain focused on their constituents and local issues.
- **Enhancing Electoral Integrity:** By limiting the influence of out-of-state money, states can work towards more equitable and representative electoral processes, ensuring that elections aren't decided by the highest bidder but by the candidate who genuinely represents the people.

Restoring Local Voices in Local Elections

The integrity of state elections is paramount for a functioning democracy. As seen in the Missouri scenario, the disproportionate influence of out-of-state donations can distort this integrity, placing local values and needs at risk. By implementing thoughtful reforms, we can ensure that state representatives truly reflect and respond to the interests of their constituents, not just those of distant donors. How would changing the rules on out-of-state donations impact your confidence in your local elections? Do you believe such reforms would lead to better representation for your community?

FIVE

AFFORDABLE LIFE

CHAPTER 32

Why is the City Transportation Not Free?

Imagine you live in a busy city where your job, the grocery store, and your favorite cafe are all miles apart. Public transportation is essential—it connects you to jobs, social events, and services. But what happens when the cost of a simple bus ride becomes too much?

The Cost of Riding

In some cities, the cost of a bus or subway ride has gone up a lot. Let's say Sarah has a family of four. For her family, the ride costs add up quickly which makes it harder for her to afford other essentials like food and rent. Why does this happen, and what does it mean for people living in the city?

Expensive Fares Hurt People With Limited Income

When public transportation is expensive, it affects everyone, but it hits people with limited incomes the hardest. They may have to:

- **Spend more of their budget on transportation**, leaving less for other needs.
- **Choose longer, less convenient routes** to save money.
- **Skip important trips altogether**, like going to a job interview or a medical appointment.

A Cycle of Economic Inequality

Expensive public transport can make economic inequality even worse. If you can't afford to get to a good job, it's much harder to improve your situation. This creates a cycle that's tough to break and can impact entire communities.

A Closer Look at Transit Economics

At first glance, transit fares seem like a straightforward way for cities to fund public transportation. However, this perspective misses the broader economic and social benefits of making city transportation either very affordable or entirely free.

The Limitations of Fare-Based Revenue

Consider the current model where transit systems rely heavily on fare revenue. This model often leads to a cycle of fare increases and service cuts when budgets are tight. Yet, fare revenue typically covers only a fraction of the total cost of operating transit services, with the rest coming from local, state, and federal subsidies.

The Economic Ripple Effect of Free Transit

When people are freed from the cost of travel, they are more likely to use public transportation for all sorts of activities:

- **Increased Retail and Entertainment Spending:** With easier access to local businesses, people may spend more on shopping, dining, and entertainment, boosting sales tax revenue.
- **Enhanced Job Access:** Free or low-cost transit removes a barrier to employment, allowing people to take jobs further from home. This can lead to higher employment rates and, consequently, more income tax revenue.
- **Tourism Boost:** Cities with free public transportation become more attractive to tourists, who then contribute to the local economy through spending on hotels, meals, and attractions.

Getting Around is Essential in Society

Though the prospect of free public transit is enticing, it comes with logistical challenges such as potential overcrowding and maintaining quality service. However, the social and economic upsides make it a worthy consideration. Imagine the freedom of boarding a bus or train without worrying about the cost. How could free public transport reshape your daily routine and your city's economy? What changes would you see in your community?

CHAPTER 33

Why Does it Cost Money to Take Money Out from Your Own Bank?

Imagine you're driving through the Sierra Nevada mountains on a snowy day. You are required to use chains on your tires. You are stopped by the road authorities. You need to pay $20 to install the chain. You don't have that much cash. You turn around, take an exit and withdraw $20 from an ATM. A few days later, you see your bank statement and notice that a $3 fee tacked onto your transaction—a whopping 15% just to access your own money! You also lived paycheck to paycheck so your bank is overdrawn. You have a $35 overdraft fee.

Banks have increasingly eliminated ATMs to cut costs and forced customers to use another bank's ATM. While this might seem like a big deal until you're hit with an extra charge just for accessing your own money. These out-of-network ATM fees can really add up, especially for people who can't afford to lose even a few dollars.

Why Paying to Use Your Own Money Doesn't Make Sense

For people living in areas without easy access to their bank's ATMs, or for those who often need cash in different places, these fees can take a big bite out of their budget. It seems especially unfair to people who have limited income, who feel the pinch of every dollar spent.

Think of Ashley, a single mother living in a small town with limited access to her bank's ATMs. To withdraw cash for her daily needs, she often resorts to using an out-of-network ATM at the local convenience store. Each transaction costs her an additional $3.50, a fee imposed by her bank plus a surcharge from the ATM owner. Over a month, these fees add up, significantly denting her already tight budget.

Understanding the Fee Structure

Banks charge these fees for a few reasons. They say it costs money to maintain ATMs and the network that allows you to access your account from almost anywhere. But when you're charged $3 or more just to get $20 out, it's worth asking: Are these charges fair?

- **Bank Fees:** Many banks charge their customers a fee for using an ATM operated by a different bank.
- **ATM Operator Surcharges:** The company or entity that owns the ATM often charges an additional fee, which can vary widely depending on the location and operator.

What Can Be Done?

1. **Banking Reforms:** Regulate banks to abolish ATM fees, especially if the bank balance is less than, let's say $10,000.
2. **Expansion of ATM Networks:** Encourage banks to expand their ATM networks or enter into agreements that allow their customers to use a wider array of ATMs without incurring additional fees.
3. **Consumer Awareness:** Educating consumers about avoiding ATM fees, such as cash-back options at grocery stores.

The Broader Implications

Imagine living in a big city where everything you need isn't within walking distance. Without affordable public transportation, you might not be able to get to your job, visit friends, or even go to the doctor easily. This is why public transport is so important—it connects people to opportunities.

This issue disproportionately affects individuals in rural areas or urban neighborhoods where specific banks do not have a strong presence. Moreover, people who work irregular hours may find it difficult to access their bank's ATMs during operating hours, forcing them to incur these costly fees. In a society where access to cash still matters, shouldn't getting your own money be simple and free? As you think about the impact of ATM fees, consider how such financial barriers might be limiting not just your own economic freedom, but also that of others in your community. How might changes in this area improve overall economic activity and fairness?

CHAPTER 34

Why Can't SNAP be Restricted to Promoting Healthy Eating?

You're at the grocery store, your cart half-filled with groceries covered by your SNAP (Supplemental Nutrition Assistance Program) benefits. As you stroll down the aisle, you grab some soda and snacks—quick, tasty, and, yes, packed with sugar. It's easy to choose these items because, well, SNAP doesn't restrict them. But here's a concerning thought: what if government programs like SNAP are unintentionally encouraging unhealthy eating habits by allowing purchases of sugary drinks and snacks that contribute to long term health issues?

SNAP provides crucial support to millions of Americans, helping families and individuals afford food each month. While

SNAP is a lifeline for many, its policies on food purchases have sparked debate, especially regarding the allowance of purchases deemed unhealthy, like soda and junk food. SNAP program is directly responsible for soda's company's billions of dollars of revenue. This underscores how the SNAP program benefits the producers of unhealthy drinks while putting millions of poor people's long term health at risk.

The Unintended Consequences of SNAP Choices

SNAP is vital for millions, providing essential food purchasing power. However, its leniency in allowing purchases of high-sugar and low-nutrition items is becoming a public health issue. This policy might be inadvertently responsible for rising rates of obesity, diabetes, and other diet-related diseases, particularly in low-income communities that rely heavily on these benefits.

Government's Role in Dietary Choices

Right now, SNAP's policy indirectly promotes the consumption of unhealthy foods by subsidizing purchases that include sugary drinks and snacks. These items are cheap and filling, but their long-term costs to health are high. By not steering beneficiaries towards healthier options, SNAP contributes to dietary habits that are hard to break and that lead to chronic illnesses.

Impact of Current SNAP Policies

Every day, families on SNAP are faced with food choices that have implications far beyond their immediate satisfaction. The easy availability and affordability of unhealthy food options on SNAP are creating generations accustomed to diets that make sickness almost inevitable. Without changes, these patterns will persist, perpetuating cycles of poor health and high medical costs that strain individuals and the healthcare system.

Rethinking SNAP for Healthier Outcomes

To break this cycle, it's crucial for SNAP to evolve from a mere food assistance program into a force for positive dietary change. Here's how:

1. **Restrict Unhealthy Options:** Implement restrictions on sugary drinks and snacks to shift purchasing patterns towards healthier alternatives.
2. **Incentivize Nutritious Purchases:** Expand initiatives like providing additional benefits for buying fruits and vegetables, making healthy food not just an option but an attractive one.

Responsible Reform

Transforming SNAP into a program that actively promotes health could significantly impact public health, particularly for vulnerable populations. It's time for policymakers to consider how SNAP can do more than just alleviate hunger—it can be a tool for nurturing healthier communities. If you or one of your friends or relatives are using the SNAP program, do you think it will be good for overall health if the sugary, junk and processed foods options are removed? Do you think by removing unhealthy food options, companies will be more incentivized to produce natural food?

CHAPTER 35

Why Can't Single Family Homes be Allowed to be Owned by American Citizens Only?

Imagine you're starting a family. You've got a steady job, your husband is working too, and together you're dreaming of buying your first home where you can raise your kids and build your future. But there's a huge obstacle in your path: despite your hard work and savings, every time you make a bid on a house, you find yourself outbid by non-citizens who pay way above the market price. You're not just competing with other families in your neighborhood; you're up against big money from non-citizens or corporations. How does that make you feel? It's frustrating and disheartening, right? This is the reality for many young American families today.

The dream of homeownership is becoming increasingly elusive for many Americans, particularly young people just starting their careers and families. Two critical issues contribute to this growing gap: the impact of non-citizens buying real estate and the stagnation of wages compared to the skyrocketing prices of homes.

Most Basic Human Needs: Food and Shelter

Home represents more than just a physical structure—it's a cornerstone of stability, security, and community for young families. However, these young people often face significant barriers for many reasons:

- **Student Debt:** The burden of student loans limits their financial flexibility significantly.
- **Entry-Level Wages:** Being relatively new to the workforce means their earnings are typically lower, making it harder to compete in a heated property market.
- **Wage Stagnation:** Even if you are an experienced professional, your wages are not growing at the top of housing prices primarily because of expanded demand of home buyers, especially non-citizens and corporations.
- **Escalating Home Prices:** Driven by foreign investment and speculative buying, the cost of homes continues to climb, pushing the dream of homeownership out of reach for many.

Government's Role is to Prioritize Citizens' Needs

The role of the government is to frame policies that first and foremost benefit its citizens. This poses a crucial question: should policy favor American companies building and selling homes in a free market to anyone, or should it ensure that American families are not priced out of their own housing market?

Capitalism Versus Necessity

While a capitalist market argues for selling to whoever will pay the most. Housing, as a basic need, demands thoughtful regulation:

- **Essential Needs:** Unlike luxury items, housing is a fundamental human requirement. Ensuring that young families can afford homes should be a priority over serving the investment interests of the wealthy.
- **Community Stability:** Communities thrive when families can plant roots. High turnover and numerous vacant homes can lead to deteriorating neighborhoods and less cohesive communities.
- **Supporting Young Families:** By making housing more accessible to them, we foster an environment where future generations can flourish.

A Case for Citizenship in Homeownership

Given these challenges, one proposed solution is to restrict home ownership to citizens only. This policy could have several benefits:

- **Leveling the Playing Field:** By limiting competition from non-citizens and corporations, home prices could stabilize, making it more feasible for American citizens to purchase homes.

- **Encouraging Investment in Communities:** Encouraging homeownership among residents who will live in and contribute to their communities can foster stronger neighborhood ties and civic engagement.

Understanding the Impact

Imagine you are in your 30s and looking to buy a house but you are outbid all the time because the price the sellers get you cannot pay. You see non-citizens and some corporations bidding on the house. What would you do? Do you think if only citizens are allowed to purchase a house, you will be able to buy one?

Homeownership is an essential step in securing your future and contributing to community stability. It's time for a balanced approach that considers the needs of American citizens, ensuring that the dream of homeownership isn't reserved only for the highest bidder but is accessible to all who aspire to it. This isn't just about economic policy—it's about safeguarding the American dream for every family.

CHAPTER 36

Why Can't Single Family Home Prices be Restricted to Wage Growth Rate?

You've been diligently working for years, saving up from every paycheck with the dream of buying your own home. Despite following all the financial advice, each year, the prices in the housing market seem to climb higher, always just out of reach. It's a frustrating reality many face today: the goal of homeownership is slipping away, not for lack of effort, but because wages simply can't keep up with the rapidly increasing costs of homes.

Wages are Stagnant But Home Prices Keep Rising

Across many regions, the price of single-family homes has surged, while wages have remained relatively stagnant. This widening gap poses a significant barrier for average Americans, particularly those early in their careers, making it increasingly difficult to secure a place to call home. The dream of owning a home is becoming an elusive fantasy for those who are left contending with an unaccommodating market.

Impact of Stagnant Wages on Homeownership

Consider a young professional couple ready to start a family and settle into a home. They're the epitome of financial responsibility: stable jobs, controlled spending, and a solid savings plan. Yet, the target keeps moving. Each year, home prices in their desired community increase faster than any raises they receive, turning their homeownership dream into a seemingly impossible goal.

As wages stagnate and home prices continue to soar, prospective buyers find themselves dedicating a growing portion of their income to mortgage payments. This creates a ripple effect, where families are forced to cut costs in other critical areas like food, education, or healthcare. It leaves them vulnerable, with depleted savings and limited financial flexibility. The additional stress of mortgage payments may prevent them from building a safety net for emergencies or saving for their children's education.

Why Linking Home Prices to Wage Growth Makes Sense

Tying the increase in home prices to wage growth could recalibrate the housing market to ensure fairness and accessibility. Here's how this could help:

- **Affordability:** It would keep home ownership attainable for the average person, preventing the market from skewing towards only the affluent or investment-driven buyers.
- **Economic Stability:** Stabilizing the housing market can lead to broader economic security, reducing the number of people overstretched by financial demands.
- **Social Equity:** This approach would allow more individuals to participate in home buying, a traditional path to building personal wealth.

The American Dream is Slipping Away

Most home buyers rely heavily on their paychecks to cover mortgage payments. If wages don't grow sufficiently to match rising home prices, more Americans will be priced out, and homes will be bought by those with deeper pockets—often non-citizens, investors or corporations. This competition leaves regular citizens unable to afford homes in their own communities, robbing them of the American dream of homeownership and contributing to a cycle that leaves working families increasingly marginalized.

Building a Fairer Housing Market

Every American deserves to buy a home at some point in their life. It used to be much earlier, mostly in 20s but now even in 30s and 40s it is not realized. By ensuring home price increases are in step with wage growth, we can create a fairer market where homeownership remains within the grasp of more Americans, supporting not just individual dreams, but the collective stability and prosperity of our society. Since most Americans buy houses on mortgage and make the payments from their paycheck, do you think you would have been able to buy a house sooner?

CHAPTER 37

Why Can't Childcare Be Free?

Imagine you're a parent of two young kids. You and your wife work full-time jobs to make ends meet. Every morning, you drop your children off at daycare before heading to work. Despite both of you working, the cost of childcare has left you with no savings. You're constantly worried about how you'll manage to pay for everything. This isn't just your problem; it's a widespread national issue that affects millions of families across the United States.

In discussions about the economic future of the United States, two points often emerge. First, the challenge of worker shortages in various industries and the concern over an aging population. Second, the simultaneous debates about immigration policies focus on how opening borders could boost the consumer base and workforce. However, an equally important solution is frequently overlooked: encouraging families to have more children by making childcare more affordable.

The High Cost of Childcare is a Barrier to Family Growth

For many potential parents, the astronomical cost of childcare is a significant deterrent to starting or expanding their families. It's not just about the immediate financial strain; it's about the long-term economic viability of raising children in an environment where both parents often need to work. If the goal is to encourage population growth and ensure a stable future workforce, addressing the childcare crisis is essential.

Fully Funded Childcare

What if the government could remove this barrier? Imagine a system where the government covers the full cost of childcare, providing parents with an estimated dollar amount sufficient to cover comprehensive childcare expenses such as food, diapers, books, toys, clothes, and children's activities. To make it super simple, the government can send a check to a family, let's say, $1000/month per child until the child reaches 16. This funding would enable parents to enroll their children in any childcare facility or educational institution of their choosing, ensuring that all children, regardless of their parents' income or background, receive high-quality care and education from the earliest stages of life.

The Argument for Universal Childcare Support

Supporting families with fully funded childcare is not just a social welfare issue; it's an investment in America's future. With adequate support, parents could more comfortably consider having more children, contributing to population growth and ensuring a robust, dynamic future workforce. Moreover, universal access to quality childcare and education would help level the playing field for all children, giving them a strong start in life regardless of their family's financial situation.

Many will argue against government-funded childcare, viewing it as an undue financial burden on taxpayers. However, this perspective is shortsighted and overlooks the broader implications of current spending habits. Here is why:

1) **Government Expenditures on Non-Citizens:** Annually, the government spends billions of dollars towards welfare programs that benefit non-citizens, including education, healthcare, food, and shelter. If such significant resources can be dedicated to this aspect of non-citizen welfare, investing in childcare—a foundational element that benefits primarily citizens—should be seen not only as reasonable but as a priority that supports the very fabric of our society.

2) **Corporate Interests in Population Growth:** Corporations invest millions in lobbying efforts to ensure a continuously growing consumer base, advocating policies that expand the population through both legal and illegal immigration. Their goal

is straightforward: a larger, younger population translates to increased consumption and profits.

3) **Corporate Dependency on Young Consumers:** The emphasis on attracting young consumers is evident in the marketing strategies and product development priorities of major corporations. They benefit immensely from a demographic that is financially supported enough to participate actively in the economy. Government-funded childcare would contribute to this demographic's growth by easing the financial burdens on families, thus enabling better early childhood development and, consequently, creating more capable and financially stable future consumers.

In light of these points, opposing government-funded childcare on the grounds of fiscal responsibility ignores the substantial long-term economic and social benefits such investments would yield. Furthermore, it highlights a significant inconsistency: we are willing to support the economic strategies that benefit non-citizens and corporate interests but hesitant to invest similarly in our own future generations. True fiscal responsibility should include preparing for a robust, well-supported youth capable of sustaining and growing our economy."

The Economic and Social Benefits

Fully funded childcare could lead to a range of positive outcomes, including:

- Increased workforce participation by parents, especially mothers.
- Enhanced child development and readiness for school.
- Greater financial stability for families, leading to increased consumer spending and economic growth.
- Support for the demographic renewal of the population, ensuring a balance between young and old.

Will You Have Kids if You Were Not Cash Constraint?

Fully funding childcare and early education would address several critical challenges simultaneously: worker shortages, demographic shifts, and the economic pressures on families. It's a bold move, but one that could secure a prosperous, vibrant future for the next generation of Americans. If you have two young kids, are you struggling to pay rent, mortgage, kids tuition or deciding whether to buy toys during Christmas? Do you think kids are the future of America and we should educate them, train them and feed them and prepare to become better citizens no matter what their economic background is?

CHAPTER 38

Why Can't Families with Kids and Expecting Mothers Get Priority in Parking?

Imagine you're at a busy shopping center. Your arms are full with bags and your toddler's hand tightly in your grasp. As you navigate the packed parking lot, every step from the far reaches of the space to the store feels increasingly daunting. This situation is all too common for expecting mothers and families with small children, where a simple outing turns into a logistical challenge. This chapter argues for the necessity of dedicated parking spots to aid these individuals, enhancing both safety and accessibility in public spaces.

Understanding the Need

- **Physical Strain**: Pregnancy brings discomfort and mobility challenges. Close parking spots significantly reduce the physical strain on expectant mothers, making it easier to run errands without added stress.
- **Safety for Children**: Parking lots are risky for young kids. With cars constantly moving, navigating these spaces can be dangerous. Priority parking closer to entrances minimizes the risk of accidents and enhances safety for families.
- **Convenience**: Managing children, groceries, and personal belongings is tough. Conveniently located parking spots make these tasks less stressful and more efficient, allowing parents to focus on their children instead of the logistics of the parking lot.

Community Insights and Experiences

- **Retail Success Stories**: Stores that implement "parent and child" parking spots near entrances receive positive feedback and increased patronage. Customers appreciate the thoughtfulness, leading to higher satisfaction and loyalty.
- **Healthcare Facilities**: Some hospitals and clinics offer priority parking for expectant and new mothers, reducing the stress of medical visits. This simple accommodation can make a significant difference in the healthcare experience for families.

Why Priority Parking Makes Sense

- **Responsible Society**: Providing dedicated parking spots shows that we acknowledge and address the unique challenges faced by these groups. It aligns with broader societal goals of equality and accessibility.
- **Public Safety**: Designated parking minimizes the risks associated with navigating parking facilities, making public spaces safer for everyone involved, particularly young children and expectant mothers.
- **Economic Benefits**: Businesses offering prioritized parking often see a return on investment through increased visits from families who appreciate the convenience. This can lead to greater customer satisfaction and loyalty.

Building a Responsible Society

Some might argue that offering special parking privileges could seem unfair to others. However, like providing ramps for wheelchair users, this initiative is about adjusting resources to meet specific needs, enhancing accessibility for everyone. Prioritizing parking spots for families with young children and expecting mothers is not merely about convenience—it's about creating a supportive, inclusive urban environment that recognizes and responds to the needs of all its residents. If you are a new mom or expecting a baby, do you think it would be helpful if the closest parking space at a grocery store door would be very helpful? How about when you visit a restaurant with your three kids?

CHAPTER 39

Why Can't Schools Be a One Stop Place for Parents and Children?

Imagine dropping your child off at a school where they can learn math & sciences, splash in a swimming pool, create a painting, learn to play martial arts, practice singing & dancing – all in one place. While it sounds simple, there are many places like this. As parents, you are often budgeting your time and money to put your children into different programs.

The Current State of Early Education

The typical journey of a preschooler might involve separate trips for different educational and developmental activities.

For instance, morning sessions at a daycare, midday swimming lessons, followed by an afternoon at a music school. This fragmented approach is not only inefficient but also places a significant burden on parents and fails to capitalize on the potential of holistic early childhood education. This not only strains logistical planning for parents but also adds unnecessary stress to young learners.

Traditional early education focuses primarily on basic literacy and numeracy, frequently overlooking the equally important areas of sports, music and dance. This oversight can lead to unbalanced growth in young children who benefit immensely from a diverse range of learning experiences including:

- **Cognitive Development:** Through reading and problem-solving activities.
- **Physical Skills:** Through swimming, dancing, and general physical education.
- **Creative Skills:** Through drawing, music, and play.
- **Social Skills:** Through group activities and structured social interaction.

Challenges with the Current System

Parents face multiple challenges with the current early education model:

- **Logistical:** Coordinating schedules and transportation to various locations for different activities (e.g., daycare, swimming lessons, music classes).

- **Financial:** Covering high costs associated with multiple learning programs and institutions.
- **Quality Inconsistency:** Encountering varying levels of quality and effectiveness across different learning settings and providers.

The Financial and Emotional Toll

Consider the financial impact on families juggling fees for multiple programs alongside their regular expenses. Then there's the emotional toll on children, who must adapt to various caregivers and teachers, which can affect their sense of security and learning consistency.

A Unified Early Education Center

Imagine a single, comprehensive early education center where children can learn to read, write, engage in arts, and participate in physical activities like dance and swimming. This center would provide:

- **Holistic Development:** Unified programs that promote all aspects of development, ensuring children grow into well-rounded individuals.
- **Convenience:** Parents drop their children off at one location where all educational activities take place.
- **Cost Efficiency:** Reduced total cost for parents, eliminating the need to pay multiple providers or for private lessons.

Will Unified Center Compromise Quality?

Some may argue that specialized institutions provide better quality in specific disciplines. While this can be true, the benefits of a unified approach—reducing the strain on family schedules and enhancing the cohesion of a child's educational experience—can outweigh the drawbacks, particularly when high-quality, integrated curriculums and trained staff are in place.

Education or All-Rounders?

Creating schools that serve as comprehensive learning centers meets the time-demanding needs of today's families. It's about training the youngest citizens not in segments, but as whole beings. This change could ease daily stresses for families, foster a more interconnected sense of community, and build a foundation for lifelong learning. Think about the young families in your neighborhood. How would an integrated education center benefit them? Could this be the key to more balanced, competitive, and happier communities?

CHAPTER 40

Why Can't Parents be Allowed to Send Their Kids to Whichever School They Want?

Imagine you have a child who is exceptionally bright. You see their potential every day. But because you live in a low-income neighborhood, you're forced to send them to a poorly rated school. This isn't just your story—it's the story of many families across America. The quality of education varies drastically based on where you live. Children in disadvantaged neighborhoods often attend underfunded schools, limiting their potential and perpetuating cycles of poverty. This story is common across the United States, where zip codes often determine the quality of education a child receives. What if parents could choose the best school for their child, regardless of their address or income?

America needs a universal school voucher system that provides educational funding directly to families. This can enable parents to choose the best educational setting for their children, be it public, private, or charter, anywhere in the country.

Current Challenges in Education

Education inequality is stark.This is because of the bureaucratic practice of tying children to their parent's wealth rather than their abilities. Children who are born in poor neighborhoods attend poor schools and earn poor salaries if they finish school. If you are born in a poor neighborhood, your fate is largely determined by:

- **Geographic Disparities:** Students' educational opportunities are largely determined by their zip code. Those in affluent areas have access to well-funded, high-quality schools, while those in economically disadvantaged areas often attend schools lacking in resources and outcomes.
- **Socioeconomic Barriers:** The current public school districting system ties school funding to local property taxes, inherently disadvantaging students in poorer districts.

- **Limited Mobility:** Families seeking better educational opportunities outside their assigned districts often face bureaucratic hurdles or prohibitive costs.

Universal School Vouchers

Imagine a scenario where every child in the United States is given a voucher worth $2,000 per month to attend any school of their choice, public, charter, or independent. The government fully funds this voucher, ensuring it's universally accessible, irrespective of a family's income or wealth. A school voucher system may entail the government providing parents with a voucher equivalent to the amount it spends per student in the public school system. This voucher could be used to fund the child's education at any school that meets state educational standards. Here's a deeper look into how such a system could transform the educational landscape and foster a fairer, more effective schooling environment.

Key advantages include:

- **Enhanced Equality of Opportunity:** Vouchers would democratize access to high-quality education by ensuring that financial resources are no longer a barrier to attending the best schools.
- **Increased School Accountability and Quality:** Schools would need to compete for students and funding, driving them to improve their educational offerings and customer service. This healthy competition fosters a culture of excellence and

continuous improvement, benefiting students and educators alike.

- **Flexibility and Choice for Families:** With the financial power to choose, parents are no longer confined to their local school districts. Parents could choose schools that best fit their children's needs, whether those needs are academic, religious, or based on extracurricular interests.

- **Enhanced School Funding and Quality:** The voucher system injects substantial funding into the educational sector, with schools receiving $2,000 per student per month. This influx of funds would enable schools to enhance their resources, hire qualified teachers, and incorporate advanced teaching tools and methods. Moreover, with schools now competing for students—and the accompanying voucher funds—they have a strong incentive to boost performance and improve outcomes to attract and retain students.

Economic and Social Benefits

- **Breaking the Cycle of Poverty:** Children from underprivileged backgrounds often find themselves in low ranked schools, lacking access to the quality education necessary for breaking out of poverty. By allowing students from low-income families to attend high-performing schools, vouchers can play a crucial role in breaking the cycle of poverty.

- **Stimulating Innovation:** Competition can lead to innovation in educational practices and methodologies, benefiting students across the board.

Universal Vouchers Increase Access to Quality Education

Implementing a universal school voucher system represents a bold step towards education choices in the United States. It empowers parents, boosts student achievement, and stimulates systemic improvements in education quality. By fundamentally rethinking how education funding is allocated and used, the U.S. can ensure that all children, regardless of their economic background or geographic location, have access to the best possible education. How might a universal voucher system help your children? Do you live in a neighborhood that does not have good schools but your child is really bright in education? What would you do if you were given the voucher?

CHAPTER 41

Why are Security Deposits So Expensive?

You've found the perfect apartment or need a rental car for a much-needed getaway. You've budgeted for the rent and the rental fee, but then you're blindsided by a security deposit that can be equal to or even triple your initial estimate. Suddenly, your plans aren't just a stretch—they're financially overwhelming.

Security deposits are a common practice in various sectors, from residential rentals to car rentals. These deposits are intended to cover potential damages or breaches of contract by the renter. However, the often exorbitant amounts can be a significant barrier for individuals with limited financial resources, effectively locking them out of essential services.

This chapter delves into the punitive nature of high security deposits and advocates for the implementation of regulatory caps.

Understanding Security Deposits

Security deposits serve as a financial safety net for providers against potential damages or contract breaches. Here's how it generally breaks down:

- **Rental Cars:** It's not uncommon for a rental company to place a hold of hundreds, sometimes thousands, of dollars on your credit card. This isn't just a formality; it can significantly reduce your available credit limit, affecting your financial flexibility.
- **Apartments:** In many cities, landlords may ask for a deposit ranging from one to three months' rent. For many, this upfront cost is the tallest hurdle to securing a home.

The Impact on You

The strain of these deposits extends beyond just a financial pinch:

- **Financial Strain:** This isn't just about the discomfort of parting with a large sum of money. For many, especially those with limited money, these funds are not spare but diverted from essential daily needs or emergency savings.

- **Barrier to Entry:** For someone in immediate need of housing or a vehicle, these costs can prevent access to essential services, exacerbating already challenging situations.
- **Dispute Anxiety:** The fear of losing a significant deposit can deter you from disputing charges even when you believe they are unjustified. This imbalance can leave you feeling powerless and unfairly treated.

Bad Companies and Landlords Try Not to Refund Deposit

Not all deposit situations stem from well-intentioned precaution. Some landlords and rental companies have developed a pattern of withholding security deposits as a steady revenue stream. By meticulously inspecting returned vehicles or properties, they find or even exaggerate minor issues to justify keeping the deposit, essentially profiting from what should be a refundable safeguard. These unethical practices not only tarnish the industry but also disproportionately affect renters with limited resources, leaving them financially drained and distrustful of future rental transactions.

Consider the story of Emily, who rented a car for a week-long trip and was careful to return it in perfect condition. Yet, she was charged for scratches she's certain didn't occur during her rental period. Fighting the charge meant possibly losing hundreds from her deposit, with no guarantee of a fair resolution.

Or take the case of Michael, a tenant whose landlord withheld half his deposit for what was described as excessive wear and tear. The cost to contest the landlord's assessment legally was nearly as much as the amount withheld.

Why Deposit Caps Make Sense

Introducing caps on security deposits could:

- **Ease Financial Pressure:** Reasonable limits on deposits would make essential services more accessible, and less of a financial burden. Caps are set at a reasonable percentage of the rental rate, say, not exceeding $500 for apartments or a fixed amount for rental cars.
- **Increase Fairness:** With regulated caps, the playing field between consumer and provider becomes more even, reducing the potential for exploitation.
- **Encourage Better Service:** Caps might also push service providers to maintain and document the state of their assets more diligently, knowing they can't rely on hefty deposits to cover costs.

The practice of requiring high security deposits needs a fresh evaluation. These funds, meant as a precaution for providers, have ballooned into significant barriers for consumers, especially those less financially secure. By instituting deposit caps and improving transparency and fairness in the handling of these funds, we can make essential services more accessible and less burdensome. Have you ever lost out on an apartment or foregone a rental car because the security deposit was prohibitively expensive? How would a change in policy regarding these deposits have impacted your decision? How did it impact the ability to access necessary services, and what changes would you propose to improve the system?

CHAPTER 42

Why Can't We Lower Healthcare Costs Instead of Debating Who Will Pay for it?

Imagine you are at a campaign rally. A politician argues that healthcare should be free. The government should pay for it, he says. Another politician says individuals should pay for it. The audience nods along. Among them is Linda. Her father just had heart surgery, and she's drowning in bills. Next to her is Mark. He's a small business owner choosing between health insurance for his employees and keeping his business afloat. These are real people with real struggles. Their problems go beyond who foots the bill. The real issue is why healthcare costs are so high in the first place.

When politicians talk about healthcare, they often argue about who should pay for it. But they miss the point. They sidestep the real problem: the high costs of healthcare. By focusing only on who pays, politicians ignore the real issue. If we made healthcare affordable for everyone, we could stop these endless debates.

Unpacking U.S. Healthcare Costs

Despite spending more on healthcare per person than any other developed nation, Americans don't enjoy better health outcomes. Here's what's driving up the costs:

- **Administrative Complexity**: The healthcare system in the U.S. is tangled in a web of administrative overhead with its numerous payers and convoluted billing systems.
- **High Pharmaceutical Prices**: Drugs cost a lot more in the U.S. than elsewhere because of patent issues, lack of price control, and intense marketing by drug manufacturers.
- **High Salaries for Medical Professionals**: Medical professionals in the U.S. earn significantly more than their global peers.
- **Technology and Overutilization**: There's a high tendency to use expensive medical technology and an approach to healthcare that favors excessive treatment.

Technological Advances vs. Healthcare Costs

In many sectors, technological advances lead to lower prices and increased accessibility. For example, over the past few decades, the costs of consumer electronics like phones, laptops, and TVs have significantly decreased while their quality has improved. This price drop is largely due to advancements in technology, economies of scale, and competitive markets that incentivize efficiency and cost reduction.

However, the healthcare sector seems to defy this economic logic. Despite remarkable technological advancements in medical science and health technologies, the costs of healthcare services have not fallen; instead, they have soared. This anomaly raises critical questions about the underlying economic and regulatory frameworks governing healthcare. Unlike consumer electronics, where market competition drives down prices, the healthcare market is tangled in a web of regulations, patents, and practices that often limit competition and obscure pricing mechanisms. Additionally, the unique nature of healthcare, where consumer choice is often limited by necessity and urgency, further complicates the dynamics that typically lead to cost reductions in other industries.

This discrepancy underscores the need for targeted reforms that not only embrace technological innovations but also overhaul the regulatory and competitive landscapes to make healthcare more like other sectors where technological advancements have led to better products at lower prices.

Making Healthcare Affordable

American don't care about political grandstanding. They want to know why healthcare is so expensive and how to make it more affordable. Shifting our focus from who pays for healthcare to why it is so expensive could change this experience. By addressing the root causes of cost inefficiency, we can make healthcare more affordable and accessible. Here's how:

Make It Efficient and Clear: Cutting down on paperwork and making prices transparent would save a lot of money. Imagine knowing exactly how much a treatment costs before you get it, just like when you buy anything else.

Control Drug Prices: Setting limits on drug prices would stop them from being so expensive. This would make important medicines affordable for everyone.

Fair Salaries and Necessary Treatments: Doctors should be paid fairly, but their salaries shouldn't be way higher than i other countries. Also, focusing on necessary treatments can lower costs without hurting the quality of care.

Debating Affordability, Not Who Pays

By shifting the focus from who pays for healthcare to why it is so expensive, policymakers can begin to address the root causes of cost inefficiency. This involves direct price interventions and broader reforms that encourage efficiency, transparency, and fairness. Next time you hear politicians debating healthcare, ask yourself: Are they addressing the real issue?

SIX

IMMIGRATION

CHAPTER 43

Is Everyone Born in the United States a Citizen by Birth?

Maria crosses the border into the United States illegally. Soon after, she meets Daniel. They have a son, David. David automatically becomes a U.S. citizen. This story isn't unique.

Every year, many non-citizens, whether they've crossed borders without authorization or overstayed their visas, give birth in the U.S. Their children get citizenship right at birth. These parents give birth to children largely in hopes of becoming American citizens one day when the child is able to sponsor the parent. Additionally, the parents successfully argue in court that they should be allowed to stay in America because their child is a U.S. citizen.

Understanding Birthright Citizenship

People born on United States soil have been getting citizenship automatically. However, this policy, intended to ensure rights and protections for the children of freed slaves post-Civil War, now faces scrutiny under modern circumstances.

Examples That Fuel the Debate

In addition to Maria's example above, who crossed the border illegally and gave birth to a son, there are numerous other ways people secure citizenship for their children. Some examples include:

1. **Giving Birth After Overstaying Visas:** Consider Anna from the Philippines, who enters the U.S. on a student visa. Near the end of her visa period, she discovers she's pregnant and decides to remain in the U.S., ensuring her child will secure citizenship. Her child's citizenship becomes a potential pathway to her own permanent residency.

2. **Giving Birth While On Work-Related Residency:** Raj and Priya, a couple from India, are in the U.S. on work visas. During their stay, they have a son, Arjun. While their initial intent wasn't to circumvent immigration laws, Arjun's citizenship provides a potential future foothold for permanent family residency.

3. **Giving Birth As a Tourist:** Li Wei travels from China under a tourist visa specifically to give birth in the U.S., a practice known as "birth tourism." Her child's U.S. citizenship is a strategic decision, aimed at securing a range of educational and social benefits available in the United States.

The Supreme Court's Role in Clarification

The rising number of such cases brings to light the need for the Supreme Court to revisit and clarify the application of birthright citizenship, particularly addressing whether it should extend to children of non-citizens who are in the country illegally or temporarily. Some suggest aligning more closely with other developed nations, where at least one parent must be a citizen or a permanent resident for automatic citizenship to be granted to a child.

Elimination v Reform

The call to eliminate or reform birthright citizenship suggests several alternatives, such as granting citizenship only when at least one parent is a U.S. citizen or permanent resident. This approach aims to align citizenship with a more direct connection to the legal and civic community of the United States. Do you think anyone born in the United States is a US Citizen? Is there a consistent abuse of the system?

CHAPTER 44

Why Can't Non-Immigrant Visitor Visas Become Easier?

Raj has been visiting the United States for the past five years on a visitor visa. He has families in both India and the United States. Raj travels frequently to visit his relatives in the United States. Raj is in the US when his visa is about to expire. He starts worrying whether he will get a visa again at the embassy in India. He has done nothing wrong but the fear gets him. He wants to make sure he is able to see his relatives again. He decides to overstay his visa.

Understanding the Motivation Behind Visa Overstays

A significant factor contributing to visa overstays is the fear among visitors that once they leave the United States, they may not be allowed to return, even if they possess multi-year visas. This apprehension is rooted in the perception that re-entry into the U.S. is uncertain, prompting some to extend their stay beyond their visa limits, hoping to maximize their time in the country.

The decision to overstay a visa is often influenced more by psychological factors than by a disregard for U.S. laws. Many visitors develop strong personal and professional ties during their stay, and the prospect of being barred from returning can seem like a significant loss. The current system inadvertently encourages overstaying by creating an atmosphere of uncertainty about future entries.

Relaxed Visa Rules

Imagine a shift in policy where the U.S. immigration system automatically reassures visitors: follow the visa rules, and your re-entry will be straightforward. Under this system, adherence to the visa deadline would significantly enhance the likelihood of hassle-free re-entry. Moreover, visitors would be acutely aware that overstaying will render them permanently ineligible to live in the U.S., effectively deterring them from violating their visa terms.

Benefits of Relaxed Visitor Visa Policy

A more transparent and visitor-friendly visa policy could yield significant benefits, including:

1. **Increased Travel:** If people are assured that compliance leads to an easier return, more visitors will be willing to travel, boosting international tourism.
2. **Increased Business Revenue:** International visitors contribute to the economy through their spending, and businesses benefit from their presence through transactions and new opportunities.
3. **Tourism Revenue:** Relaxed policies could lead to a surge in tourism revenue, supporting local economies and businesses that rely heavily on visitor spending.
4. **Stronger Family Connections:** Easier travel would strengthen family bonds by allowing families to visit each other more frequently, reducing overstays driven by the fear of separation.
5. **Reduced Overstays:** By reassuring visitors that compliance leads to smoother future visits, a relaxed policy could significantly reduce the rate of visa overstays.

Enforcing Compliance with a Balanced Approach

Easing visa rules could significantly alleviate the fear of separation and uncertainty surrounding re-entry, but a balanced approach requires strong measures to enforce compliance and maintain the integrity of U.S. immigration laws:

- **Immediate Deportation:** Any individual caught overstaying their visa would be subject to immediate removal from the United States, ensuring that those who break visa rules face immediate and tangible consequences.

- **No Benefits**: Overstaying a visa would mean complete ineligibility for any U.S. benefits, assistance programs, or public services, preventing visa violators from accessing resources.
- **No Appeal or Remedy**: Individuals overstaying their visas would not have the right to appeal their deportation or seek legal remedies. This no-exception policy would emphasize the seriousness of the violation, eliminating any opportunity to prolong their stay or challenge the decision.
- **Permanent Re-Entry Ban**: Overstaying would result in an irrevocable lifetime ban on entering the U.S. again, serving as a powerful deterrent to those considering overstaying their visa. Such stringent measures would signal to all potential visitors that compliance is crucial.

Creating a Welcoming, Compliant Environment

By understanding and addressing the fears that lead to visa overstays, the U.S. can foster a more welcoming and compliant environment. This isn't about leniency but about intelligent policy-making that recognizes human behavior and adjusts to it constructively. Such an approach respects visitor aspirations while maintaining the integrity of U.S. immigration laws, striking a balance between openness and regulation. How would knowing that following the rules ensures easier future travels affect your view on visiting the U.S.? Do you think this approach could decrease visa overstays?

CHAPTER 45

Why Do You Need H1B Work Visas in the Era of Remote Work?

A leading technology company in San Francisco, like Google, posts a job opening for a Software Engineer. In today's world, where remote work has become a norm rather than an exception, this position does not require the employee to physically present in the office. Jaideep, a talented developer from India, applies and secures the job. Interestingly, he is required to relocate to San Francisco under the H1B visa program, despite the fact that he hardly ever visits the office and could have easily performed all his duties from India, where Google also maintains a significant presence. This scenario prompts a crucial question: In an era where the job can be effectively performed from anywhere in the world, what is the justification for the H1B visa, especially when physical presence at the workplace is no longer a necessity?

The H1B visa program, designed to allow U.S. employers to hire foreign specialty workers temporarily, has been a cornerstone of tech industry hiring practices for decades. However, the global shift towards remote work, accelerated by the COVID-19 pandemic, calls into question the future necessity of this visa category. With increasing numbers of employees working remotely, this chapter argues for a reevaluation of work visa policies to better align with the current economic and technological landscape.

Understanding H1B Visas

The H1B visa is intended for specialized occupations that require theoretical or technical expertise, notably in fields such as IT, finance, engineering, and medicine. While this program helps fill gaps in the American labor market, it also ties the employee's residency status to their employer, creating a dynamic that many critics argue is exploitative.

The Rise of Remote Work

The pandemic has irreversibly changed perceptions about workplace norms, proving over the course of the pandemic for several years that many jobs can be performed from virtually anywhere. This shift has significant implications for the H1B visa:

- **Geographical Irrelevance:** Employees no longer need to be physically present in the U.S. to contribute effectively to their teams.
- **Cost Reduction:** Companies can reduce overhead costs associated with physical office spaces while employees save on commuting and living expenses in high-cost urban areas.
- **Global Talent Pool:** Employers can access a broader talent pool without the legal and logistical complexities of immigration.

Implications for H1B Visa Policy

- **Decreased Necessity for Physical Presence:** The need for H1B visas may diminish as companies realize that the location of their employees is less relevant than their ability to perform tasks effectively.
- **Potential for Exploitation:** The linkage of visa status to employment may become increasingly unnecessary and could be seen as a means of binding employees to specific employers under potentially inequitable conditions.
- **Economic Impact on Developing Countries:** Allowing foreign workers to remain in their home countries while working for U.S. companies can lead to economic benefits globally, as these employees contribute to their local economies rather than the U.S. economy.

A Global Workforce for a Global Economy

The traditional model of tying work visas to physical presence in the U.S. is becoming increasingly outdated. By embracing remote work and restructuring visa regulations, the U.S. can enhance its competitive edge by tapping into global talent efficiently and ethically. This approach not only benefits U.S. employers and their international employees but also contributes to global economic stability. Are you currently working with remote colleagues in foreign countries? If they are in the United States, how often do you meet them in-person? Is there truly a need for people to leave their home country for a job that could be done remotely?

CHAPTER 46

Where is More Fraud in Immigration? Marriage or Employment Based Petitions?

Elena, a student from Spain studying in the U.S. on a student visa, meets Jack, a U.S. citizen. They fall in love, and after college, they decide to marry. Jack files a petition with the U.S. government for Elena to receive a green card (USCIS Form I-130). However, their marriage is automatically viewed with suspicion, as the government assumes that marriage-based green cards could be used to "game" the system. Consequently, Elena is issued a two-year conditional green card and must file a waiver later to prove that her marriage to Jack is genuine.

In contrast, Jay works as a grocery clerk. Another grocery store, Yummy Foods, submits a petition (USCIS Form I-140) to sponsor Jay for a permanent position. Jay receives his green card without any conditions but soon leaves for a job at Walmart.

There are two common ways for people to obtain green cards: marriage and employment. Marriage-based green cards are scrutinized intensely because of fears that these relationships are strategic ploys for residency. On the other hand, employment-based green cards are seen as less susceptible to deceit. This chapter questions this paradox and examines whether employers, employees, or the system itself are responsible for misleading the U.S. government.

Neither the Employer Nor Employee is Truthful

You want to check with your friends if they got their Green Cards based on employment? Are they still working at the same company that told the US Government it has a permanent offer? It is highly unlikely. In filing the petition, who was untruthful, the employer or the employee or both? What does permanent offer mean and for how long does the employee need to be employed by the petitioning employer?

Marriage-Based Green Cards: Rigorous Scrutiny

The U.S. Citizenship and Immigration Services (USCIS) implements rigorous checks for marriage-based green card applications, including interviews meant to ascertain the authenticity of the marital relationship. The scrutiny is intense, driven by the belief that marriages could be contrived for immigration purposes. However, despite the skepticism, many of these marriages are built on genuine relationships and shared lives.

Employment-Based Green Cards: No Oversight

Conversely, employment-based green cards are often perceived as straightforward and fraud-free. The process involves a U.S. employer sponsoring a non-U.S. worker based on permanent employment offers. Nonetheless, it's not uncommon for employees to leave their sponsoring employers shortly after receiving their green card. This raises questions:

- **Employee Motivation:** Are employees committing to these roles in good faith, or are they using the employment offer as a stepping stone to residency?
- **Employer Complicity:** Are employers aware of the transient intentions of their employees? If so, to what extent are they complicit in facilitating what might be seen as a deceitful practice?

Examining the Discrepancies

The high rate of job changes among sponsored employees suggests a mismatch between employee intentions and the "permanent" offers stated in their petitions. This raises several concerns:

- **Systemic Incentives**: What defines a "permanent employment offer," and how long must an employee stay? Marriage-based green cards come with a two-year conditional requirement, while employment-based green cards do not.
- **Regulatory Oversight**: Unlike marriage-based green cards, post-approval checks for employment-based green cards are minimal.

Who is Deceiving Whom?

Enhanced post-approval checks are essential for employment-based green cards. This leads to a critical question: who is misleading the U.S. government—the employer, the employee, or both working together to 'game' the system for green cards?

SEVEN

DAILY NONSENSE

CHAPTER 47

Why are So Many Lanes Closed for Minor Accidents?

Imagine you're cruising along on your way to work, music playing, morning coffee in hand, when suddenly traffic grinds to a halt. Up ahead, four lanes are blocked off by law enforcement due to a minor accident that realistically affects only one lane. This over-utilization of resources not only disrupts your morning commute but also raises significant questions about the efficiency of traffic management during such incidents.

Excessive Resource Use in Traffic Management

In many cities, the response to minor road incidents often seems disproportionate to the actual situation. Here's what you might observe:

- **Overly Aggressive Lane Closures:** An entire section of a highway is shut down for an accident that, by all appearances, could have been managed with far fewer restrictions.
- **Extended Traffic Delays:** These broad closures lead to massive bottlenecks, significantly delaying hundreds, if not thousands, of commuters.
- **Disrupted Lives and Economies:** The ripple effects extend beyond just the road, impacting schedules, fuel consumption, and even local businesses that rely on timely arrivals and departures.

The Need for Proportional Response

The key issue here is the lack of proportionality in the use of law enforcement and traffic management resources. Overreaction not only strains resources but also saps public trust in city management. Citizens often feel that such measures are more about exerting control than ensuring safety.

Balancing Safety with Sensibility

Effective resource management should aim to balance the need for safety with the practical realities of city life:

- **Targeted Lane Closures:** Limit closures to directly affected areas to minimize broader impact.
- **Enhanced Traffic Flow Strategies:** Employ traffic management technologies and strategies that adapt in real-time to changing conditions on the ground.

A Smoother Road Ahead

The goal should be to create a system where road safety protocols are as minimally invasive as possible while still maintaining high safety standards. By focusing on effective resource management and proportional responses, cities can ensure smoother commutes and less public frustration. Is it possible to manage traffic better and also provide the necessary law enforcement help? Have you found yourself stuck in traffic for hours only to notice that a minor accident happened in only one of the lanes?

CHAPTER 48

Why is Furniture Assembly So Complex?

You've just picked up a sleek new bookshelf that's supposed to be the final touch for your living room. The box is surprisingly compact, the price was unbeatable, and now, all that's left is to put it together. But as soon as you open the box and spread out dozens of screws, panels, and the cryptic instruction manual, your afternoon project suddenly feels like an overwhelming ordeal. This scenario is all too common with flat-pack furniture, which promises convenience but often leads to frustration.

Why Flat-Pack Furniture Can Be So Tricky

Flat-pack furniture has revolutionized how we buy and transport home furnishings. Brands like IKEA have mastered the art of cost-effective, stylish designs that you can take home today and use tonight — theoretically, at least. But once the box is open, the reality of assembly kicks in:

- **Complex Instructions**: Ever felt like you need a degree in engineering to follow furniture assembly instructions? You're not alone. Many manuals provide vague steps or lack sufficient diagrams.
- **Unexpected Tools and Parts**: Discovering you need a specific type of screwdriver or wrench halfway through the process can be a real headache, not to mention the baffling assortment of fasteners and components.
- **Design Intricacy**: As furniture design becomes more stylish and functional, the assembly process naturally grows more complicated. More features often mean more assembly steps.

The Frustration Factor

Assembling furniture taps into a mix of spatial, logical, and sometimes even physical challenges:

- **Cognitive Load**: Figuring out how all the pieces fit together without a hitch would strain anyone's cognitive abilities, especially with subpar instructions.

- **Time Sink**: What looks like a quick setup on paper often turns into hours of work, which can fray even the most patient person's nerves.
- **Physical Demand**: Wrestling with large panels or aligning multiple screws requires both strength and finesse, which can be taxing.

From Historical Necessity to Modern Headache

The concept of flat-pack furniture, initially meant to make stylish home decor accessible and transportable, has not always considered the user's assembly experience. This oversight has sometimes turned what should be a rewarding DIY project into a daunting task.

Reimagining Furniture Assembly

By rethinking how flat-pack furniture is designed, instructed, and supported, manufacturers can transform furniture assembly from a chore into a more positive, even enjoyable part of home decorating. Reflect on your own furniture assembly experiences. What were the main challenges, and how could the process have been smoother? Have you seen any innovative approaches that made putting together furniture easier and less stressful?

CHAPTER 49

Why Do Climate Change People Not Care to Clean Streets?

I magine walking through your neighborhood in San Francisco with friends who are passionate about the environment and climate change. The streets you are walking on are littered with trash. It presents a curious paradox. Many people who are vocal about climate change overlook the very dirty streets full of trash and drugs that lie right at their feet and they do nothing about it.

The Overlooked Issue of Local Cleanliness

The cleanliness of our local environment often doesn't receive the attention like the climate change agenda. One reason could be that climate change, with its media coverage, feels more urgent and compelling. Local environmental issues like street cleanliness might seem less significant or less impactful in comparison. Additionally, tackling climate change often involves high-profile glamor, media and attention, which can be more appealing than the less glamorous task of picking up trash.

Integrating Local and Global Efforts

The enthusiasm for tackling global climate issues should be mirrored in our local environmental actions. The litter that accumulates in our streets doesn't just stay there; it often finds its way into rivers and oceans, contributing to global pollution. By caring for our immediate environment, we are taking actionable steps that have both local and global benefits.

The Significance of Local Environmental Actions

Addressing the cleanliness of our streets is not just about aesthetics; it's about public health, community well-being, and the protection of local wildlife. Trash on our streets can lead to greater environmental degradation, affecting water quality and contributing to broader ecological problems.

- **Public Health**: Dirty streets can harbor harmful bacteria and attract pests, posing health risks to the community. For example, in 2018, San Francisco faced a public health crisis due to the accumulation of human waste and used needles in public areas, which contributed to the spread of diseases.

- **Environmental Impact**: Local litter often ends up in waterways, contributing to ocean pollution. A study by the National Oceanic and Atmospheric Administration (NOAA) found that a significant portion of ocean debris originates from urban areas, highlighting the link between local litter and global pollution.

The Significance of Local Environmental Actions

The neglect of local cleanliness by some climate change advocates is a strategic oversight that undermines long-term environmental goals. It is difficult to explain why big environmentalists shy away from cleaning their own streets. What is the quality of your street? Is it dirty? Are environmentalists there to clean often?

CHAPTER 50

Did Paper Straw Advocates Think of Little Kids?

Imagine you're out with your three-year-old at Starbucks. You get her favorite drink, and it comes with a paper straw. After just a few minutes, you notice her struggling as the straw bends, softens, and eventually collapses into a soggy mess. She starts chewing on the paper and swallowing it. Paper straws were meant to solve the environmental problem posed by plastic straws, but this well-intentioned switch didn't fully account for the practical issues that young children might face. This advocacy for eco-friendly alternatives sometimes leaves families frustrated, and it's worth exploring what lessons we can learn.

The Appeal of Paper Straws

Paper straws emerged as a biodegradable solution to the plastic waste cluttering our oceans and landfills. With their compostable nature and renewable materials, they seemed like the perfect alternative. Their appeal quickly led many restaurants, cafes, and food vendors to make the switch, with environmental organizations promoting them as a way to help save the planet.

Challenges of Paper Straws for Kids

Despite their good intentions, paper straws present real challenges for kids (and parents too):

- **Durability Issues**: Children often take longer to finish their drinks, and with paper straws that break down in liquid quickly, this often leaves them with a crumpled straw that barely functions. You might find yourself frequently needing replacements.
- **Chewing Hazards**: Kids have a tendency to chew on straws, and paper straws can easily break into small bits, which poses a choking hazard or leads to accidental ingestion of paper pieces.
- **Chemical Exposure**: Some paper straws are treated with adhesives or dyes, which could be harmful if ingested. With children being more susceptible to chemicals, this raises concerns about their safety.

Balancing Environmental Benefits with Practicality

Advocates of a cleaner environment lost sight of practicality and inclusivity in the process without adequately considering their functionality and safety for children. Have you noticed your little children chewing paper straw at coffee shops? Did the coffee shop understand that three years old can't use paper straw?

CHAPTER 51

Why Can't You Get Good Customer Service These Days?

Remember the good old days when you walked into a store and were greeted with a warm smile and a helpful "How may I assist you today?" Those days seem like a distant memory now, replaced by hurried "Next!" and interactions that feel as cold as the automated systems we often navigate from our screens. This shift isn't just in your head; it's a real change that has been sweeping through industries worldwide.

The Decline of Customer Care

- **Technological Automation**: Take the example of a recent flight delay. You rush to the customer service desk, only to be directed to a self-service kiosk or an automated phone system. These technologies were designed for convenience and cost reduction. However, they've stripped away the personal touch that once defined customer service.
- **Changing Consumer Expectations**:With the rise of digital culture, the emphasis has shifted towards speed and efficiency. Many consumers now prioritize quick service over personal interaction. For example, if you are shopping inside Walmart and you need help with a a product, it is extremely difficult for you to find one associate which suggests they force you to buy online and discourage visiting their store.

Reflecting on Service Experiences

The decline in customer service standards is not just a business trend but a strategic error that can undermine long-term success. Businesses need to reinvest in the foundational aspects of customer care—respect, courtesy, and personal attention— that can distinguish them from the competition and build lasting customer loyalty. When customers have a choice, they have a long memory of bad customer service. Think about a recent positive or negative customer service experience. What made it memorable, and how could either scenario have been improved? What do you value most in customer service interactions?

CHAPTER 52

What's the Need of Construction in the Busy Day Time?

Think about the last time you were stuck in traffic because of road construction. The frustration of inching forward, brake lights glowing ahead, and the impatience building with each passing minute. You weren't alone in feeling annoyed and inconvenienced by the gridlock. Construction work in the middle of the day not only makes your commute miserable but also disrupts businesses, impacts local economies, and strains public patience. So why do we insist on doing road work during peak hours when shifting it to nighttime could be a game-changer?

The Daily Gridlock

- **Traffic Congestion**: Daytime roadwork often happens during peak travel hours, turning your route into a maze of cones, barriers, and reduced lanes. Traffic slows to a crawl or even stops, leaving you and other drivers stuck in long delays.
- **Economic Costs**: The more time you spend idling on the road, the more fuel you burn and productivity you lose. Businesses are also affected as deliveries are delayed and employees show up late.
- **Environmental Impact**: Your car idling in bumper-to-bumper traffic contributes to more emissions, harming the environment and adding to the urban smog problem.
- **Public Safety**: With sudden traffic pattern changes and heavy machinery nearby, navigating around work zones can be risky for both drivers and pedestrians.

Advantages of Nighttime Roadwork

- **Reduced Traffic Impact**: With fewer cars on the road at night, crews can work more quickly and efficiently without constantly stopping for vehicles.
- **Increased Worker Safety**: Less traffic means fewer hazards for construction workers, keeping them safer while they do their jobs.
- **Improved Quality of Work**: Cooler temperatures at night are often better for certain construction materials, helping workers do a better, longer-lasting job.

- **Public Convenience**: You can travel more smoothly with fewer roadblocks and fewer headaches when you drive during the day.

The Story of the "Big Dig" in Boston

One of the most notable examples of the benefits of nighttime construction is the "Big Dig" in Boston. This massive infrastructure project involved rerouting the central artery of Interstate 93. Initially, the daytime construction caused severe traffic congestion and public outcry. When the project shifted significant portions of the work to nighttime, traffic flow improved dramatically during the day, and the overall project timeline was reduced. This shift not only alleviated daily commuter frustrations but also showcased the effectiveness of nighttime construction in a major urban area.

Switching to Night Time Work

- **Mandate Nighttime Roadwork**: Encourage or require that major road projects in urban areas happen at night, except for emergencies.
- **Invest in Technology**: High-quality lighting and quieter machinery can make nighttime work safer and quieter.
- **Public Communication**: Clearly inform the public about construction schedules and traffic changes well in advance.
- **Monitor and Evaluate**: Continuously gather public feedback to refine night time road work practices.

Weighing the Trade-offs

The switch to night time road work offers a sensible solution to a problem that impacts many cities around the world. Shifting construction to off-peak hours means less congestion, improved safety, and happier commuters. As cities weigh the benefits and challenges, it's important to consider how you and other residents will feel the impact. How would this change improve your daily commute, and what can be done to make the transition easier for workers and residents alike? How would a shift to nighttime construction impact your daily life, and what steps can cities take to make this transition seamless for both workers and residents?

CHAPTER 53

Why are Sports Stadiums in the Busiest Areas of a City?

Picture the last time you tried driving through the city on a game day. You were likely stuck in bumper-to-bumper traffic as throngs of sports fans crowded the streets, the stadium visible in the distance as the source of your frustration. With noise and traffic reaching unbearable levels, you might have wondered: "Why do we put these huge stadiums in the busiest parts of our cities?"

The Realities of Central Stadium Locations

- **Traffic Congestion**: You've seen the chaos firsthand. Thousands of fans converge on the stadium, overwhelming city roads and creating gridlock that paralyzes the city. Take the example of Dodger Stadium in Los Angeles. On game days, the nearby freeways and streets are often clogged, causing massive delays not just for fans, but for everyday commuters as well.

- **Public Transit Strain**: If you've ever tried to take public transit on game day, you know how crowded it gets. The sudden surge in passengers makes it tough for regular commuters to get around. In New York, the 7 train to Citi Field can become almost unbearable, packed with Mets fans, leaving little room for daily riders.

- **Quality of Life**: Noise, disruption, and litter can make living near a stadium frustrating. Residents often feel like their own neighborhood has been invaded. For instance, residents around Wrigley Field in Chicago frequently deal with rowdy crowds and increased litter, impacting their daily lives.

- **Economic Displacement**: Some local businesses near the stadium thrive on game days, but others, unrelated to sports, see a drop in customers as traffic becomes impassable. In Seattle, businesses near CenturyLink Field (now Lumen Field) have noted mixed impacts, with some benefiting from game day crowds while others suffer from decreased accessibility.

Historical Context

Traditionally, city planners built stadiums in urban centers to ensure easy access and to benefit from existing infrastructure.

This made sense in an era when cities were more compact, and public transportation systems were designed to funnel people into centralized areas. However, as cities have grown and transportation methods have evolved, the issues stemming from central stadiums have become increasingly hard to ignore.

Advantages of Outskirts Stadiums

- **Easing Traffic Congestion**: Building stadiums on the city's outskirts can help manage game-day traffic better and keep the downtown core moving. Look at AT&T Stadium in Arlington, Texas, home of the Dallas Cowboys. Located outside the busy urban areas of Dallas and Fort Worth, it reduces the traffic burden on the central business districts.

- **Tailored Infrastructure**: On the outskirts, there's space for ample parking and traffic management systems that won't interfere with regular city traffic. Levi's Stadium in Santa Clara, California, was designed with extensive parking and transportation infrastructure to accommodate large crowds without disrupting the nearby urban centers.

- **Enhanced Fan Experience**: More room outside the city means stadiums can expand with better facilities and easier access. For instance, MetLife Stadium in East Rutherford, New Jersey, offers extensive amenities and easier access compared to older urban stadiums, providing a more comfortable experience for fans.

- **Economic Development**: Outskirts stadiums can stimulate regional development and create job opportunities where they're most needed. The development around Gillette Stadium in Foxborough, Massachusetts, has spurred local economic growth, bringing new businesses and jobs to the area.

A Strategic Shift

Moving stadiums to the outskirts requires a strategic shift but can alleviate many challenges tied to urban stadiums. There are potential trade-offs, such as ensuring adequate transportation options for fans who want to attend games. However, modern infrastructure planning can address these concerns.

- **Public Transit Solutions**: Cities can develop dedicated transit lines or shuttle services to connect urban centers with outskirts stadiums. The success of such systems can be seen with the light rail service to University of Phoenix Stadium in Glendale, Arizona, which efficiently moves fans without causing downtown congestion.
- **Economic Considerations**: While some businesses may miss out on game day traffic, the overall economic benefits of reducing congestion and improving quality of life for residents can outweigh these drawbacks. Furthermore, new business opportunities can arise in the areas surrounding the new stadium locations.

A Strategic Shift

The placement of sports stadiums in the busiest parts of our cities presents numerous challenges, from traffic congestion to the strain on public transit and the impact on local residents' quality of life. By considering a strategic shift to placing stadiums on the outskirts, cities can alleviate these issues while promoting economic development and enhancing the fan experience. Imagine how much smoother your city could run on game days without the gridlock and chaos. It's time to rethink where we place our sports stadiums for the benefit of all. What are the potential trade-offs of moving stadiums to city outskirts? Can the people who want to watch a game still visit the stadium easily?

EIGHT

EXCESSIVE REGULATIONS

CHAPTER 54

Why Do You Need Licenses for So Many Small Businesses?

I sis Brantley was a hair braider from Texas. For years, she braided hair without any issues, until one day, she was arrested for practicing without a cosmetology license. She had to fight a lengthy legal battle to continue her work. Her story highlights a significant issue: the overwhelming and often unnecessary licensing requirements for many small businesses.

The Over-Regulation of Professions

Imagine you're passionate about braiding hair, arranging flowers, or running a food truck, and you want to turn your passion into a livelihood. But as you take steps to start your business, you're hit with licensing requirements that feel unnecessarily stringent and costly. You're not alone in feeling this frustration. In recent years, licensing laws have ballooned, making it challenging for many small businesses to operate without jumping through endless hoops.

- **Excessive Hours**: You're required to undergo hundreds of hours of education, often at significant expense, just to shampoo hair or arrange flowers. For a profession with minimal safety risk, this seems like overkill.

- **Economic Impact**: These licensing requirements can create significant financial barriers to starting a small business, restricting your entry into the field and reducing competition. This leaves only a few providers who can charge high prices while keeping out lower-income entrepreneurs.

- **Examples of Excessive Licensing**: You might relate to florists in Louisiana who need to pass a licensing exam, casket sellers in Oklahoma who are heavily regulated, or hair braiders across states facing licensing barriers despite little public safety risk.

The Case for Reform

- **Aligning Requirements with Risks**: Licensing standards should only require training that matches actual health and safety risks. This way, you're not forced to spend unnecessary time and money on irrelevant certifications. For example, reducing the training hours required for hair braiders to focus solely on what they need to know would be more reasonable and practical.

- **Economic Benefits**: Scaling back these barriers can open up job opportunities and reduce the cost of services for consumers. This benefits both you and your potential customers. When Utah eased licensing restrictions for hair braiders, it allowed many entrepreneurs to start their businesses, increasing competition and lowering prices for consumers.

- **Enhanced Mobility**: Standardized license requirements across states can help you move your business across state lines, ensuring your skills are valued wherever you go. This is particularly important for military spouses who frequently relocate and struggle with varying state licensing laws.

Promoting Economic Opportunity

You deserve a fair shot at building your business without being buried in paperwork and costly licensing exams. By reducing unnecessary licensing, states can unlock economic opportunity for small business owners like you, helping you grow your passion into a successful, thriving enterprise. For example, Patricia Edwards from Tennessee wanted to open a home-based bakery. However, the state's stringent licensing requirements, including a commercial kitchen, made it nearly impossible for her to start her business. After much advocacy, Tennessee passed the Cottage Food Law, allowing Patricia to bake and sell from her home. This change opened doors for many home-based entrepreneurs like her.

Government Should Make Starting Business Easy

We can balance safety and economic opportunity for everyone. Licensing requirements are meant to protect consumers, but when they become overly burdensome, they stifle innovation and entrepreneurship. Is a licensing requirement holding you back from realizing your dream? What would you do?

CHAPTER 55

Why Do Businesses Need to Pay Franchise Tax Every Year?

Jane is a young entrepreneur with a dream. She opened a small coffee shop in her small hometown. She poured her savings, time, and heart into opening the business. Despite all her efforts, the business is running at a loss for the first few years. She does not have investors and she doesn't know how she will keep the lights on. Then she gets the annual franchise tax bill in the mail.

Every year, Jane pays $800 just for the privilege of running her coffee shop, regardless whether she makes any money or not. This fee made it tough for her to break even, let alone grow her business. Jane feels like this tax as an unfair burden that keeps her from putting her hard-earned money where it's needed most.

The Weight of Franchise Taxes

Franchise taxes are imposed by some states on businesses to grant them the legal right to operate. This isn't like income tax, where you pay based on what you earn. No, this tax is a flat fee, calculated through complicated formulas involving your assets or net worth. It's money out of your pocket no matter how well—or poorly—your business is doing.

The Disproportionate Impact on Small Businesses

- **Financial Strain**: For small businesses like Jane's boutique, every dollar counts. The $800 franchise tax meant less money for essential expenses like marketing, inventory, and repairs. In slower months, this fee could make the difference between staying afloat and closing down.
- **Administrative Burden**: Calculating the franchise tax can be a headache. Jane often needed to hire an accountant just to make sure she got it right. That's another expense and more stress on top of everything else.
- **Competitive Disadvantage**: Unlike large corporations, small businesses don't have the financial cushion to absorb these extra costs easily. This puts them at a competitive disadvantage, as larger

companies can handle these expenses without much trouble. Or if you're building a tech startup that hasn't yet generated any revenue. You are struggling to raise venture capital money and you are chasing angel investors every day to fund your startup. If you are successful in raising investor money, you can then pay the franchise taxes.

Questioning the Necessity of Franchise Taxes

- **Lack of Direct Benefits**: When you pay franchise taxes, what do you get in return? Unlike other taxes that fund infrastructure or services, franchise taxes feel like a fee for simply existing. You're paying just to keep your doors open.
- **Economic Inhibition**: These taxes can stifle innovation and entrepreneurial spirit. Small businesses are the backbone of our economy, driving job creation and growth. Burdening them with unnecessary taxes hampers their ability to thrive and contribute to the economy.
- **Unnecessary Financial Strain**: For businesses like Jane's boutique, the annual franchise tax is an unnecessary financial strain. Instead of helping her grow her business, it acts as a barrier to success.

Alternatives and Reforms

- **Threshold Exemption**: Imagine if smaller businesses and startups were exempt from franchise taxes until they hit a certain revenue or profitability level. This would give them a chance to grow before being burdened with additional costs.

- **Reduced Rates for Startups**: What if we had a graduated tax rate that increased as your business became more financially stable? This would help new businesses get off the ground without being weighed down by high initial costs.

- **Allowance for Reinvestment**: Picture being able to reinvest what you would have paid in franchise taxes back into your own growth. This could be used as a credit for expenses like marketing, hiring, or expansion.

Supporting Business Growth

Franchise taxes disproportionately affect small businesses and startups, the very entities that can least afford them. By reevaluating these fees and considering alternatives that support growth, we can foster a healthier entrepreneurial environment. Imagine the impact on your business if these taxes were reduced or restructured to help you grow rather than hold you back. Do you think franchise taxes create any value for your company?

NINE

SOCIAL ISSUES

CHAPTER 56

Is Affirmative Action Benefiting the People for Whom It Was Created?

You are an academically competitive young Black man from Louisiana, and you apply to Harvard. You think you have a good chance of getting admitted since you are a Black American whose ancestors were slaves and will be favored under Affirmative Action. You find out that you have been rejected. Your spot likely went to someone who applied from Nigeria, raising the question: Is Affirmative Action truly helping those it was originally meant to help?

Why Was Affirmative Action Created?

Back in the 1960s, during the Civil Rights Movement, the U.S. government created Affirmative Action to address the historical injustices faced by African Americans due to centuries of slavery, segregation, and systemic discrimination. The policy aimed to provide opportunities that had been historically denied to certain communities, especially Black Americans. By encouraging the inclusion of underrepresented groups in education and employment, Affirmative Action sought to create a more diverse and inclusive society. This involved providing access to higher education, employment, and other areas where minorities had been historically underrepresented, helping them achieve social and economic mobility.

Drift from Original Intent

The application of Affirmative Action over the decades has broadened significantly. Today, the policy covers a wide array of minority groups, some of whom may not have faced the same systemic discrimination intended to be addressed by the original measures.

Contemporary Challenges and Misapplications

In recent years, a contentious debate has emerged about the beneficiaries of Affirmative Action. Critics argue that the policy now often benefits individuals who broadly fall into the minority category but do not necessarily belong to the groups that were the primary targets of historical injustices in the

United States. This expansion has led to complexities in implementation, with some key points being:

- **Dilution of Benefits**: The extension of benefits to a broader array of groups has potentially diluted the effectiveness of Affirmative Action for the descendants of slaves, who were the principal intended beneficiaries of these policies.
- **Competition for Limited Resources**: As more groups are included under the Affirmative Action umbrella, competition for limited slots in educational institutions and job opportunities has intensified, sometimes at the expense of the very groups these policies were designed to help.
- **Perceptions of Fairness**: There is growing debate on whether Affirmative Action as currently implemented is fair to all people, including those from non-minority backgrounds who are unjustly disadvantaged by these policies.

Distinguishing Affirmative Action for Black Descendants of Slaves or Any Black

While Affirmative Action was originally designed to rectify the disadvantages faced by descendants of American slaves, the broad application of these policies today often does not distinguish between African Americans with slave ancestry and those without. Prominent figures like Barack Obama and

Kamala Harris provide insightful case studies for this discussion.

Barack Obama's father was Kenyan, and his mother was a white American from Kansas. Although Obama identifies as African American, he does not have ancestors who were slaves in the United States. His familial connection to the African American experience is rooted in his identity and personal history, rather than a direct lineage to American slavery. Kamala Harris's heritage includes a Jamaican father and an Indian mother. While Jamaica's historical context involves slavery under British rule, Harris's direct connection to American slavery is non-existent. Her Black ancestry connects her culturally and ethnically to African Americans but not to the specific group that Affirmative Action was originally intended to support.

Now contrast the examples of Barack Obama and Kamala Harris with Frederick Douglass and Martin Luther King Jr. Both Frederick Douglass and MLK were not only pivotal to the civil rights movements of their respective times but also descendants of American slaves. Their advocacy and the injustices they fought against were directly tied to the legacy of American slavery—economic, social, and political disenfranchisement that Affirmative Action aimed to address.

Many have argued, perhaps rightfully so, that Obama and Harris took the spot of qualified Affirmative Action beneficiaries—at college, in jobs, and even in the office of president or vice president. The Black American descendant of slaves has yet to become America's president or vice president.

The Need for Nuanced Policy Application

The examples of Obama and Harris highlight a critical issue in the current implementation of Affirmative Action: the lack of distinction between different heritages within the broader Black American community. This conflation leads to misallocated resources and dilution of the policies' impact on the rightful beneficiaries.

Refinement

Given these challenges, there is a strong case to be made for refining Affirmative Action policies to better align with their original intent. Affirmative Action was created as a remedy for deep-seated injustices and inequalities. However, as society evolves, so too must the policies designed to foster fairness and equality. By reassessing and recalibrating these initiatives, we can uphold the spirit of the original legislation while ensuring that its benefits are appropriately and justly distributed.

What do you think would be the best way forward? Would refining Affirmative Action policies to focus more on the descendants of American slaves make a difference? How about focusing more on the economic disadvantages people face rather than their ethnicities? It's a conversation worth having—acknowledging the past while striving for a more balanced future.

CHAPTER 57

Is a One-Time Reparation Really Possible?

Imagine a young African American student named Sarah. She's working two jobs to pay for college while caring for her younger siblings. Her family has lived in poverty for generations because her ancestors were brought to the United States as slaves. Due to systemic problems against Blacks, her father was not able to own any assets, not even a basic house.

Sarah's story is a common one among American descendants of Black families. Generations have been snatched away from them. Once they were freed, segregation and unjust judicial crackdowns on Black men left many families fatherless. Blacks own almost nothing in wealth despite arriving in the land of dreams at the same time as any other American.

Now, imagine the possibility of a one-time reparation that could change her future. The real question isn't just whether reparations are possible but how to make them fair and effective.

The Reparations Fund

One approach could involve descendants of slave owners contributing to a "Reparations Fund." This fund would be designed with strict criteria to ensure fairness and accountability.

- **Historical Proof**: There must be clear, documented evidence that an individual's ancestors owned slaves. For example, historical records from plantations could provide the needed proof.
- **Benefit from Slavery**: It must be shown that the wealth of the descendants was significantly influenced by their ancestors' ownership of slaves. This might include examining old property records, inheritance documents, and family business histories.
- **Minimum Net Worth Threshold**: Only individuals with a net worth of at least $5 million would be obligated to contribute 50% of their net worth, focusing on those who have benefited the most from

historical injustices. This approach targets wealth that has been directly passed down through generations.

- **Exclusion of Post-Slavery Wealth**: The calculation for contributions would exclude wealth generated independently of slavery's legacy, focusing on inherited wealth directly traceable to the exploitation of enslaved people. This ensures fairness in how contributions are assessed.

Addressing Practical and Ethical Concerns

This proposal raises several practical and ethical questions:

- **Verification and Administration:** Establishing a robust system to verify historical records and assess individual wealth would be crucial.
- **Moral Obligations:** The moral rationale behind asking descendants of slave owners to contribute to reparations lies in acknowledging unjust enrichment at the expense of enslaved individuals and their descendants. It's an attempt to rectify the ongoing impact of that injustice. Imagine a family that built its fortune on a plantation. Their modern-day wealth could be seen as partly owed to the labor of enslaved people.
- **Economic Impact:** Critics might argue about the economic fairness of this approach. However, setting a high net worth threshold aims to mitigate concerns by focusing on those who can afford to contribute without facing financial hardship. By targeting the

wealthiest, this approach minimizes the impact on those who are less financially secure.

Use of the Fund

The "Reparations Fund" would grant a one-time payment to the descendants of slaves, providing a tangible form of compensation for historical injustices. This direct compensation to descendants of slaves can help bridge the economic gap and provide immediate financial relief. For example, Sarah's family could receive a one-time payment that allows her to invest in education, housing, or starting a business.

A Path Forward

Implementing reparations is a complex challenge, requiring careful consideration of historical context, ethical implications, and practical realities. This structured approach to reparations seeks to balance the scales of justice in a tangible, perhaps imperfect, manner. It recognizes the need for meaningful action to address the lingering effects of slavery, while also considering the fairness to descendants not personally responsible for their ancestors' actions.

America is a generous country. Perhaps those who have been advocating for reparations can consider starting the Reparations Fund. This does not require any government involvement. They could transfer a portion of their wealth to the Reparations Fund, and the Fund could start making payments to the descendants of slaves.

What do you think would be the best way forward? Would a reparations fund, as outlined, be enough to make a difference? As you think about this complex issue, consider how a meaningful dialogue could bring fresh ideas and solutions that align with your vision for justice. It's a conversation worth having—acknowledging the past while striving for a more balanced future.

CHAPTER 58

Why is it Acceptable in America to Burn the American Flag?

Imagine you are walking on the streets of New York. You see protestors vandalizing properties and burning the American flag on the street. Although you don't like seeing the American flag being burned, no one can do anything. Despite the American flag's national significance, the Supreme Court has ruled that flag burning is protected under the First Amendment as symbolic speech. This chapter argues that flag burning should be punished, not through imprisonment, but through meaningful fines that serve to deter disrespect towards this national symbol.

The Current Legal Framework

In 1989, the Supreme Court decided in Texas v. Johnson that burning the flag is a form of free speech. This means it's allowed under the First Amendment, letting people show their disagreement or criticism. Gregory Lee Johnson burned the flag outside the 1984 Republican National Convention in Dallas to protest the Reagan administration's policies. The court ruled that even offensive speech is protected under the First Amendment.

Reasons to Punish Flag Burning

- National Unity: The flag stands for our shared identity and values. Burning it can cause big divisions in society. Fining people for this act would stress the importance of national unity and respect for these common values. For example, after the 9/11 attacks, the American flag became a powerful symbol of unity and resilience. Seeing it burned could deeply hurt and divide people who see it as a symbol of national solidarity.

- Respect for Sacrifices: Many people see the flag as a sign of the sacrifices made by soldiers and civil rights leaders. Burning the flag is seen as a big insult to those who fought for our freedoms. Think about veterans who have risked their lives under this flag. To them, and many others, burning the flag is like dishonoring their service and sacrifice. During the Vietnam War, many protests included flag burning, which deeply offended many Americans, especially those with loved ones serving overseas.

- Deterrence Through Fines: Instead of sending people to jail, big fines can stop people from burning the flag. This way, we avoid the hassle of figuring out jail sentences and focus on financial penalties. In countries like Germany and France, fines for desecrating national symbols help maintain respect for those symbols while avoiding the complications of imprisonment.

The Need for Financial Penalties

Punishing flag burning with fines has several benefits:

- **Fair Punishment**: Fines are a balanced way to punish disrespect without the harshness of jail, which might seem too severe and make things worse. For instance, in Australia, fines for defacing the flag help maintain respect without creating a heavy burden on the legal system.

- **Preventing Disrespect**: Big fines would make people think twice before burning the flag, reducing the number of times it happens. In South Korea, strict penalties for flag desecration have successfully reduced such incidents, showing that strong financial deterrents can work.

- **Simple to Enforce**: Fines are easier to handle than jail time and avoid the complicated legal and ethical issues of imprisoning people for symbolic speech. This approach ensures quick and efficient enforcement.

Implementing the Change

To make this change, we need to:

- **Pass Laws**: Congress should pass laws that clearly define the fines for flag burning, making sure they are big enough to be a real punishment but not too extreme. This would require bipartisan support and clear guidelines to ensure consistency.
- **Educate the Public**: The government should explain why the flag is important and why there are penalties for burning it. Public campaigns could highlight stories of veterans and other citizens who deeply value the flag.
- **Ensure Fairness**: Make sure the fines are applied fairly and not used to target specific groups or individuals. Legal safeguards can help prevent misuse of the law and ensure that fines are applied justly.

Upholding Dignity Without Suppressing Speech

Flag burning is a controversial issue, but by using fines instead of jail, we can protect the dignity of our national symbols while still respecting free speech. This way, people can still express their views without disrespecting the flag. Would using fines instead of jail change your mind about punishing flag burning? How do you think this would affect how people see the law and the flag?

CHAPTER 59

Why is the Government Allowed to Print Any Amount of Money it Wants?

Think about running your household or business. You budget carefully to make sure you don't spend more than you earn. Now imagine if you could just print more money when you're short. While that sounds easy, it's not practical or sustainable. Governments often print money to cover their financial gaps, but doing so creates risks that can affect the whole economy.

Why Governments Print Money

You might wonder why the government prints money in the first place. They typically do it to:

- **Cover Budget Shortfalls**: When there's not enough revenue from taxes, the government sometimes creates new money to pay for its obligations.
- **Stimulate the Economy**: During economic downturns, printing money can boost spending and investment.
- **Manage Public Debt**: Printing new money helps governments meet their debt obligations, but this comes at a price.

Problems with Printing Money

While printing more money seems like an easy solution, it carries significant drawbacks:

- **Inflation Risks**: More money in circulation without a corresponding increase in goods and services leads to rising prices, reducing your buying power and making everyday essentials more expensive.
- **Debt Mismanagement**: Printing money encourages poor financial discipline, letting governments dodge tough decisions and leaving future generations to handle the fallout.
- **Undermines Confidence**: When a government prints too much money, people lose faith in the currency,

sparking financial crises and affecting international trade.

Should Governments Operate Like Families and Businesses?

If governments adopted similar principles to those of households and businesses, you might see:

- **Budget Discipline**: They would need to balance their budgets instead of creating more debt, promoting long-term stability.
- **Encourages Efficiency**: With limited funds, governments would have to use resources wisely, reducing waste.
- **Enhances Accountability**: If governments couldn't print money freely, they'd be more accountable to you, the taxpayer, for how they spend your money.

Challenges of Over-Reliance on Printing Money

While printing money can provide short-term relief, it creates long-term problems like:

- **Short-Term Fixes**: Artificial stimuli from newly printed money lead to dependency rather than sustainable solutions.
- **Public Burden**: Inflation primarily impacts everyday people, particularly those on fixed incomes, as their money loses value.

Advocating for Fiscal Conservatism

A more disciplined fiscal approach could help avoid these issues:

- **Adopting Balanced Budgets**: Pass laws to make the government live within its means.
- **Promoting Savings**: Encourage the government to save during economic booms, like you might put away money for a rainy day.
- **Transparent Spending**: Make government spending more transparent so you can see how your money is being used.

Prudent Economics

If governments operated like responsible households and businesses, prioritizing budgeting and living within their means, they could create more stable economies. This approach would help limit inflation, encourage long-term growth, and protect future generations.

What do you think about governments never printing money? What challenges might come up, and how would you address them?

www.ingramcontent.com/pod-product-compliance
Lightning Source LLC
Chambersburg PA
CBHW071924150726
47999CB00001B/95